The White Orchard

BOOKS BY ARTHUR SZE

POETRY
Into the Hush
The Glass Constellation: New and Collected Poems
Sight Lines
Compass Rose
The Ginkgo Light
Quipu
The Redshifting Web: Poems 1970-1998
Archipelago
River River
Dazzled
Two Ravens
The Willow Wind

TRANSLATIONS
The Silk Dragon II: Translations of Chinese Poetry
The Silk Dragon: Translations from the Chinese

COLLABORATION
The Unfolding Center (with Susan York)

PROSE
The White Orchard: Selected Interviews, Essays, and Poems

EDITOR
Chinese Writers on Writing

The White Orchard:
SELECTED INTERVIEWS, ESSAYS, AND POEMS

Arthur Sze

Museum of New Mexico Press
Santa Fe

CONTENTS

For Carol

There is an exchange of all things for fire,
and of fire for all things.

—HERACLITUS

OVER THE YEARS, many readers have asked me to put together a book of interviews so that people who read my poetry may better understand my cultural background, my approaches to poetry, and my creative process. I have only recently decided it's an appropriate time, and I started by looking at thirty-six interviews. There are many overlaps in them, and I selected seven and added three essays to widen the discussion. Readers have sometimes found my poetry difficult, and I believe the works selected here will provide insight and will serve as an important companion to my book *The Glass Constellation: New and Collected Poems* (Copper Canyon Press, 2021).

This present collection is divided into six sections. The first section is foundational; it opens with a short, introductory interview and then moves on to a second interview that includes a close reading of two poems, along with a rich discussion of two major poetic sequences. The second section, "Balancing Rigor and Spontaneity," juxtaposes two interviews. The first shows the influence of classical Chinese poetry on my own poetry, and it shows how I frequently work through juxtaposition to create sequences, which I call "the form of our time." The second interview deepens the discussion and also touches on my engagement with contemporary science.

Section three, "Landscape As Autobiography," features an essay that grew out of a talk I presented at the *Writing on Water* conference at Brown University in 2018. It discusses my connection to the *acequias* of Northern New Mexico. I lived in Jacona, New Mexico, for seventeen years and have lived in Santa Fe for over thirty-three years. In Jacona, I lived near the Ancon de Jacona acequia, and the title poem to my book *Sight Lines* is situated in that place, where the speaker walks in that ditch during the off-season. Since 2014, I have been involved in the Acequia del Llano in Santa Fe that starts at Nichols Reservoir and runs roughly parallel to but at a higher elevation than Upper Canyon Road and eventually drops into the Santa Fe River. In this essay, I connect the movement of water along acequias to a *quipu*, an Inca recording device. The branches of water that run downhill from the main ditch, seen from the air, resemble the hand-spun quipu with knotted cords that Incas used to record information. This poetic leap enables readers to see how I frequently make surprising connections, and the essay includes poems to show how these connections are manifest in my poetry.

Section four opens with a keynote address I gave in Washington, DC. This "Intimate Lecture" was commissioned by the Library of Congress Poetry and Literature Center and Smithsonian Asian Pacific American Center, as part of the 2019 Asian American Literature Festival. In this talk, I "walk" through contemporary Asian American literature and use personal anecdotes and readings of excerpts by other Asian American poets to show the rich diversity of Asian American poetry. I include reclamation as part of my project and read two short poems written by Japanese Americans who were incarcerated in Santa Fe during World War II. Most Americans, and certainly many New Mexicans, are unaware of this history, so my inclusion of these poems brings the overlooked, as well as the celebrated, into conversation with each other.

The next piece, "Well-Travelled Path," is an interview I did with Esther Belin, a poet, editor, and former student of mine at the Institute of American Indian Arts. Although some of the earlier interviews in this book touch on my connection to IAIA, this interview is the fullest exposition of my teaching experience there. From 1984-2006, I played a pivotal role in creating the BFA program in Creative Writing, and I mentored a generation of emerging Native poets. Many of the best-known Native poets today graduated from the Institute of American Indian Arts, and I mentored such poets as DG Okpik, who was recently a finalist for the Pulitzer Prize; Layli Long Soldier, who received the National Book Critics Circle Award; as well as Sherwin Bitsui and James Thomas Stevens, who have each received a Whiting Writers Award. In this interview, I discuss how I created the Creative Writing Program that has had such success.

In section five, I open with a second interview by poet Tony Leuzzi that focuses on my book, *Sight Lines,* which won the 2019 National Book Award for poetry, and it also includes drafts of a poem, "Kintsugi," that show my creative process. It is followed by an interview with Eileen Tabios, where I share eighty-eight drafts of my poem "The White Orchard" and discuss my creation of a new poetic form, the "Cascade." Many readers have said they find this interview particularly illuminating, because it shows how slowly and how meticulously my poems develop from the first rough draft to the final completed poem. This interview also shows how arduous and how exciting the process of writing a poem can be. The final draft of "The White Orchard" was selected for inclusion in the 2021 *Best American Poetry* as well as the 2022 *Pushcart Prize: Best of the Small Presses* anthology. This section closes with another poem, "Sleepers," and a discussion of how I created and shaped that poem.

The final section includes the two short poems and two extended sequences that are discussed in the foundational "Demolishing Hierarchy" interview, and they are included here for easy reference. It is my hope these interviews and essays will not only provide insight into my own poetry and poetics but that they will be of value in wider discussions of literature.

I · FOUNDATIONS

REVEALING AND REVELING IN COMPLEXITY:
An Interview with Arthur Sze, by Jim Natal (2022)

JIM NATAL: Do you remember the first poem you wrote? What prompted it?

ARTHUR SZE: My first semester at M.I.T. I sat in a large calculus class and felt increasingly bored by the lecture. I remember flipping to the back of a spiral notebook, and I started writing phrases to a poem. I was excited at what came to me, and, before the end of class, I had a rough draft. On a subliminal level I realized that, although I was capable at math and science, I didn't want to spend my life in that endeavor. Poetry was a leap into the unknown, and I was prompted to write by an urge to discover something that was truly meaningful to me and not follow family expectation. I wrote that first poem, then a few days later I wrote another poem. Then another. And another. I liked the compression and musicality of poetry. I knew no other form of writing that was so thrilling and compelling.

JN: Was there a teacher, family member, or other person you encountered when you were young who exposed you to poetry?

AS: Instead of a teacher or someone else who introduced me in an exciting way to poetry, I remember, in junior high school, cringing at the way the English teacher approached Coleridge's "The Rime of the Ancient Mariner." She instructed everyone in class to analyze "the albatross" and search for other hidden meanings. So my first memorable encounter with poetry was tense and negative. In that class, poetry was approached as something that was necessarily difficult, esoteric, and with a correct way to come to terms with its meanings. Later, at a private high school, I had a more sympathetic exposure to poetry. I read poems by Dylan Thomas and Yeats and remember being struck by their rhythms and musicality.

My parents were immigrants from China, and they encouraged me to write only with the understanding that writing well was an important academic and professional skill. Writing creatively was not encouraged at all. My family expectation was that I would pursue something safe and professional: scientist, engineer, doctor, investment banker. Poetry was seen as something wild and risky. Yet, my father had a classical literary education in China that rounded out his career in science in America. I remember looking at and marveling at English translations of Chinese classics in his study—translations of the *I Ching*, the *Lao-tzu*—so my literary seeds were actually planted there.

JN: Do poets need an MFA (or PhD) for their work to have credibility?

AS: I never attended or graduated from an MFA program, so I clearly don't believe an MFA is requisite to becoming a poet. Nevertheless, I did take two undergraduate poetry workshops that were crucial to my development.

My sophomore year at M.I.T. I took a poetry workshop with Denise Levertov. Denise was the first poet I met, and her passion for poetry was inspiring. She had just taught at the University of California at Berkeley, and I decided to transfer there [in 1970]....At UC Berkeley I took a poetry workshop with Josephine Miles, and she became instrumental to my development. As my faculty advisor and mentor, Josephine enabled me to create an individual major in poetry. I took Chinese language and literature classes and started to translate Tang dynasty poetry into English. To a significant extent, I learned my craft through translation. I was also lucky in that Josephine believed in me. Every two or three weeks I went to her house on a Saturday afternoon and showed her a batch of new poems. She responded to them with great care and insight, and she also directed my reading. At the end of one session she recommended Rilke, another time Neruda. It was never part of a class or for class credit—these individual sessions with her were precious and foundational to my growth.

JN: Must poets win prizes to be considered established? Are prizes a gauge of success?

AS: It would be disingenuous of me to say that prizes do not matter, because I have received many. Sometimes the cash that comes with a prize has given me precious time to write; sometimes it has given me encouragement; sometimes a prize has brought new readers to my poetry, so I am grateful for what I have received. At the same time it's important to recognize that writing poems does not depend on that recognition. If I hadn't received any awards, I would still be writing poetry. Wallace Stevens once wrote that poetry is a source of pleasure, not of honors. It's good to keep in mind Emily Dickinson who wrote and wrote, with little recognition throughout her entire life, and whose courageous body of work is a better measure of success than any prize.

JN: What moves you to poetry? Do you write to be read and published, or for yourself?

AS: I love the intensity and power of language, emotion, and imagination that all come together in poetry. It's an essential language and as necessary as breathing. It helps me live and grow in the world. Writing poems over many years involves growing and deepening and maturing as a complete human being. Solitary as this practice is, I hope that my poetry, like all poetry, speaks to others and is a gift that awakens and moves others to experience the world in profound, essential ways. And I am trying to make my tiny contribution against oblivion.

JN: Science and nature inhabit your work and, even when not the focus or theme of a poem, seem an ever-present low-grade hum in the background. How do you, as a poet, integrate the technical and scientific with the natural and organic?

AS: When I first wrote poems, I tried to avoid scientific vocabulary and structures. I was turning away from M.I.T. and the world of science and turning toward nature. But then I realized that art and science are not antithetical, as some people suppose. As paths of inquiry and understanding, poetry and science can inform and inspire each other. Since I have that scientific knowledge and training, I decided that using it in my poetry was a way to develop rigor and clarity in my writing. I suppose I integrate the technical and scientific with the natural and organic because they balance and enrich each other. Like it or not, we live in a complex, challenging world, and the scientific and the natural are endlessly entangled. I never consciously set out to integrate one with the other; maybe I realized they are already endlessly entwined, and one of my themes or obsessions has to do with revealing and even revelling in that complexity.

JN: How does pan-cultural curiosity and cross-cultural involvement influence your work?

AS: I'd like to quote Theodore Roethke: "I learn by going where I have to go." In the beginning, I translated classical Chinese poetry because I wanted to draw on my ancestry and felt I had so much to learn from those ancient poems. When I graduated from UC Berkeley, I was adventurous and wanted to go somewhere I had never been before. Josephine Miles suggested Santa Fe and gave me the name of a friend, Stanley Noyes. I hitchhiked into town forty-nine years ago, with only a backpack and my curiosity. I looked up Stan, and he suggested I apply to the New Mexico Poetry-in-the-Schools program. I did, was accepted, and worked for ten years all over the state: on Indian reservations, in Spanish-speaking communities, with incarcerated juvenile offenders, at the New Mexico School for the Deaf (with the support of a sign translator) and in the Penitentiary of New Mexico, where I even worked with an inmate on Death Row. I was excited to discover a part of America I knew nothing about, and I felt an immediate affinity with Native Americans.

When I wasn't working in the schools, for several years I also did construction work as a plasterer—how many contemporary American poets have worked with their hands?—and I learned enough Spanish so that I could read Neruda and Lorca. These steps weren't premeditated, but I wanted to expand my range of experience, and one step led to another. Phil Foss, a poet who taught at the Institute of American Indian Arts, invited me to read my poetry and teach occasional poetry workshops there. I so enjoyed meeting and teaching Native students from tribes across the United States and, eventually, although I did not have a graduate degree, I was hired and became a professor there [1984-2006].

New Mexico is a very multicultural place, and over time, my cross-cultural experiences and connections have deeply informed my poetry. I've used specific Hopi words in my poems, and I've also drawn on a social ceremonial dance at San Ildefonso Pueblo, but these usages have never felt forced. They entered my poems as part of my personal experience. I've always been interested in meeting creative people in other disciplines, and from other cultures. I have always felt I have so much to learn, and my poetry has over time reflected that growth. I don't write a poem thinking about what I can do to make my poetry unique. Instead, if I dig deep and write with openness and risk, I find that the poem I write will emerge and eventually become what it needs to be.

DEMOLISHING HIERARCHY:
A Conversation with Arthur Sze, by David Baker (2022)

DAVID BAKER: Arthur, it's a real pleasure to have this chance to talk with you. I've been a fan of your work for a long time, as you know, and we are glad to feature these two new lyric poems in *The Kenyon Review*. For our talk I think we'll start with these poems but we'll also reach back into the KR archives to talk about others of your poems that we've printed over the past several years.

I'm drawn to the powerful paradox that these two poems create, each in its way. First, I am attracted to the sharply chiseled shape of the poems. "After a New Moon" and "Returning to Northern New Mexico after a Trip to Asia" both commence with lines that feel almost like blank verse. Or perhaps they are loosely accentual, with four and sometimes five strong beats to each line. And the lines are shapely and balanced.

The paradox arises, then, when the coherence of the lineation meets the very quick-changing narrative, the dramatic or cognitive sense of things. The poems make such surprising turns. They change pronouns, they change locations, they change their patterns of image. These shifts occur almost with each new sentence. I find the tension between formality and surprise, then, to be powerful and evocative. How much of these tactics is willed, and how much is discovered or happened-upon?

ARTHUR SZE: I like to think of my writing process as a zigzag way. I often start with slivers, fragments, and try to germinate phrases and nurture the process of discovery. It's important not to know too soon where it's going—it's important to encourage and even sustain this process of suspense—but, eventually, I have so many phrases I start sifting and searching for what has urgency, what feels most alive. As I do this, I find I'm also searching for an arc, a structure, and a form begins to take shape. As I start orchestrating some of the slivers, I have a conscious tactic of writing the phrases out in two-line stanzas, where the white spaces enable me to leap more freely.

I wouldn't call these two-line stanzas couplets, because, to my mind, a couplet has a kind of integrity, whereas, in this early stage, I'm playing more with juxtaposition of phrasing and trying to keep open, in the white space, the possibility of leaping into something unexpected, or shifting tonally into another register, or, alternately, developing a narrative line that might fill in the space with a greater sense of completion. So even after I have a provisional shape to the poem, I still go back and forth between what I like to call "rigor"—inner necessity—and "spontaneity"—the possibility of discovery and surprise. Eventually, I hope to have a poem that harnesses both.

For the two poems you mention, I checked first drafts and found that in "After a New Moon," only one phrase from the first sheet of phrases, "the shifting course of a river," eventually made it, in slightly different form, into the final poem. In "Returning to Northern New Mexico after a Trip to Asia," the last phrase, starting with "Kamikaze pilots," was there at the outset, but I tried repeatedly in the early stages to make it the opening. I eventually realized it was much more effective as the end. I mention the specific genesis to these two poems because they show how the full poem is rarely there at the outset and how the tension between formality and surprise has to be earned.

DB: What do you mean "the first sheet of phrases"? You say you start with slivers and fragments. I think of Emerson's evocative statement in "The Poet" that "bare lists of words are found suggestive to an imaginative and excited mind." Is that how these poems started, as phrases and lists, in two-line groups? Do you also start with random sentences? Or something else entirely, like a sense of music or of graphic arrangement?

AS: The two poems grew in different ways. In "After a New Moon," I started with a vague pressure and wrote out a series of phrases in two-line groups. I wouldn't call them lists, because there wasn't any verticality to them. Rather, the phrases were more like charged clusters. I agree with Emerson's statement and would expand "bare lists" to "bare lists and phrases." I often play with random phrases with the feeling that they're somehow connected below surface in ways I can't see. Sometimes a sense of music propels a phrase forward, sometimes I search for a sense of line. It's a highly intuitive process. In "Returning to Northern New Mexico after a Trip to Asia," I had the last two lines very quickly and, with it, a sense of cadence and line. I also had a clear narrative impulse but pursued several narrative threads before they coalesced.

DB: Your poems—and these two are typical of this technique—frequently have a narrative coherence to them. Yet they are not stories exactly, nor do they proceed in a linear narrative. So what determines the order of the phrases and pieces? Even if the effect is of the random or the concurrent, still you are making decisions about sequence on the page.

AS: Sequencing is very important. At a certain stage, if I feel I'm in too much control, I might take a series of phrases, even the beginning and ending, and reverse their order to see if I can discover something unforeseen. Eventually, when I work out the final sequencing to a poem, I'm searching for a quality of inevitable unfolding: although there's no linear narrative, I need to feel each twist and turn is essential.

DB: The effect of shifting, of shifting phrases, as well as changing scene or image or focus, becomes part of the speaker's own self-awareness in these poems. But more so, it becomes part of his storytelling tactic. At the end of "After a New Moon" he revises himself, as if even he is surprised by the direction of thinking in his poem. It's the moon—no, it's his mind that moves from bright to dark.

Is this a form of complicity on his part, of desiring to come closer to us? Is this revision, which you have kept in the poem rather than edited out, an indication of the provisional nature of things?

AS: I believe the interruption in the next-to-last line of "After a New Moon" has several effects. First, I want to say that the disparity between intention and effect is one of the great mysteries of art. I can have an intention, or set of intentions, but the effect, or cluster of effects, may be quite different from what I expected. And that's good: a poem is often smarter than the poet. Just as the process of creation involves exercising control and releasing it, so the effects in a poem are often more powerful when they are least anticipated.

Here I want to add a distinction between superficial and deep surprise. On a first reading, a poem may dazzle with surface effects, but if the underlying rigor isn't there, the initial surprises evaporate, whereas, with a deep surprise, there may be an initial feeling of discomfort and disorientation, but over several readings, the singularity of vision and underlying rigor emerge. In this case, the surprise becomes powerful and lasting.

In creating "After a New Moon," I happened to catch the speaker in the act of asserting then revising the assertion even as he makes it. As you mention, I could have edited it out, but, instead, I felt it was what the Greeks called a *hermaion*, a gift, a lucky find. In doing so, I hoped to enact the process of qualification and discovery, rather than present the result.

I was also consciously working with a voice casting a spell, and, yes, I hoped this interruption would reveal the provisional nature of not just this assertion but of all things. The notion that this is a form of complicity, or desiring to come closer to the reader, is an important element to that rupture, but it wasn't, at least in the act of writing it, my primary concern. Nevertheless, as an unforeseen or unanticipated effect, it's a significant one.

DB: More about the provisional then. I notice and am moved by the constant flux of your poems. Nothing holds still and yet a kind of abiding peace or acceptance grows, even when the details of a poem are grim or hard. How do you think about the relation of stability to change or the provisional?

AS: I like to invoke the image of the yin/yang symbol, where, in the swirl of white, there's a black point, and, in the swirl of black, there's a white point. Darkness isn't privileged over light, and light isn't privileged over dark. Rather, the visible points inside of each swirl are the points of interconnection and transformation. I want to be paradoxically rooted in the flux of the world, and I'm drawn to the points and to the edge where light turns into dark, and dark into light. As part of this process, I'm interested in demolishing hierarchy: a butterfly opening its wings may be of equal importance as the death of a friend in a car crash. And I like to utilize equivocal contrast as a means to heighten the tension between antinomial forces and give shape to the flux.

DB: Demolishing hierarchy. Yes, I think that's a primary aesthetic, and probably political impulse in your poems. I want to return to that in a little while when we look at some of your longer poems, where the effect is even more vividly felt.

But I notice another important shared characteristic in the poems at hand. That is, their quality of after-effect. Both poems are uttered "after" an event or trip. I don't notice this trope as a frequent one in your other short poems, so I wonder if it's a new thing, or perhaps a coincidence.

The effect, though, is a powerful one. The poems come to us with a kind of gathered wisdom or a sense of experience. Something has happened and now the speaker can report. The world seems fresh, too, in each poem's after-effect—things seen with an especially clear light, whether those things are beautiful or difficult.

AS: I think the conscious harnessing of an after-effect in these two poems is new. "Returning to Northern New Mexico" was written before "After a New Moon."

Some background might be pertinent here. In November 2007, I was in Hualien, Taiwan, for an international poetry festival that was held in a pine garden retreat. As I looked out toward the Pacific Ocean, the idyllic scene was demolished when Sylvie Tang, a graduate student who assisted me as a translator, told me Kamikaze pilots spent their last days there, drinking and whoring, before launching themselves against American naval war ships.

That jolt became a seed for the poem. And, when I finished "Returning to New Mexico," I felt the trope of an after-shock could be developed more figuratively. As I worked on "After a New Moon," the interruption in the next-to-last line created the shock that reverberated through the poem. Because the two poems are each eighteen lines long, were written consecutively, deal with similar issues, even if in contrasting ways, I think of them as twins.

DB: I do, too. But there are a couple of interesting differences. In "After a New Moon" the second-person point of view also suggests an "I," a surrogate for the speaker. That's clearly the camera angle of the poem. In "Returning to Northern New Mexico" the stance is explicitly first-person. And yet the mood and mind-set of the two poems seem pretty similar. How do you think of the differences there in pronoun and point of view?

AS: I often play with shifting pronouns and point of view and believe that's part of the destabilizing and provisional nature of things. It's also a rich arena for creative exploration. In "After a New Moon," I hope the "you" is rich in ambiguity. It could be the unnamed "I" is addressing an other: a spouse, for instance; or the unnamed speaker could be addressing and struggling with an aspect of himself. If the speaker is struggling with an aspect of himself, it's possible the "I" becomes changed in the process.

DB: In your most recent previous *Kenyon Review* appearance, we printed your longer poem "Spectral Line." I think of this as one of your central recent poems. It also seems like a mini-anthology of your primary methods. These methods are compressed in "After a New Moon" and "Returning to Northern New Mexico." In "Spectral Line," with its nine sections, they are more extended.

From the first section you show your ability to combine and juxtapose—from Native American references to Buddhist sensibilities to personal and domestic narratives. As the poem proceeds, I find changes in pronoun and point of view, in stanza structure, even in a kind of syntactic method. The poem moves quickly, as in part two, then seems suspended in meditation and peacefulness, as in part three.

AS: The scientific definition of "Spectral Line" is, in small scale, a chromatic fingerprint of an excited gas, and, in large scale, a band of images corresponding to radiation emitted by a particular source. When I wrote "Spectral Line," the Institute of American Indian Arts was my source of energy, and I wanted to use the scientific meanings as an underlying, structural principle; but I was also interested in the idea of a specter haunting the imagination.

I love working in sequences, where there's room to create worlds inside the world of the poem. And I like the large-scale rhythmical possibilities a sequence affords. Section two enacts a disorienting experience of loss and needs to jar and move quickly, whereas, in section three, as you note, there's a floating stillness. In orchestrating a sequence, I'm consciously working with stillness and motion, a variety of diction and syntax, braiding narratives.

DB: One of the critical sections is section four. This is where you rip apart the syntax, suspend a need for closure, and let the stanzas hang there, connected by the mere staple of a semicolon. They aren't really stanzas, are they?

What I mean is each segment feels equivalent to each other, each is like a segment in a collage, and the effect is a kind of concurrent happening. You manage to create a feeling of non-judgment, of equanimity or acceptance—from the near-suicide to the spring apple, from the flirty secretary to the grandeur of adding to "human culture." And you end with a question. The feeling of equanimity or equivalence is important to you, isn't it? So is the resistance to closure.

AS: Yes, section four isn't really organized into stanzas. I like that you call the phrases segments. They aren't quite fragments—many are syntactically complete sentences—but they are juxtaposed to create a kind of simultaneity where linear time and consequence are suspended: It's as if anything can happen, or all things happen at once. I'm interested in incorporating a wide range of experience and creating a vast web of equivalences. A feeling of equanimity comes from a kind of release, of non-attachment, but if there was only equanimity, there would be no poem. And, yes, I'm interested in resisting closure. Instead of circling back and closing things off, I've noticed that my poems often expand, rest, then expand more, or they stop on a dime. In an earlier time, the closure of the poem may have been satisfying, but, in our world today, closure risks a premature or false sense of completion.

DB: Why do you think we resist closure these days, or, as you say, a sense of completion? Is it our modernist inheritance, our distrust of the complete, our distrust of authority? Must the vase have a crack in it?

AS: I think closure represents a kind of closing off, and, with the increasing complexities of our contemporary world, it's harder and harder to do. Closure, I think, is like the answer to a question. If someone asks a question and you can make an authoritative answer, you attain a sense of completion; but, if the answer is provisional and leads to another question, then the authority of the answer is undermined.

It is easier to employ closure if you have a linear narrative: x leads to y and eventually z is a kind of denouement. But what if the world is a ten-dimensional game of *go*? (*Go* is the Japanese name; in Chinese, it's called *wei ch'i*—where two players, alternately, place black stones or white stones on a board of crisscrossed lines and attempt to capture each other's stones by surrounding them.) If causes and effects are unseen and unclear, and a vast web is in place instead of a billiard ball view of causality, closure, completion is virtually impossible. So resistance to closure, I think, has a bit of all that you mention: modernist inheritance, distrust of the complete, distrust of authority.

I would add that my experience of the world is closer to simultaneity and to *weiqi* than to linear narration. Nevertheless, if someone asserts that the vase *must* have a crack in it, I have to object. Poetry must resist any form of coercion. If the prevailing mode is so far in the direction of open forms and resistance to closure, then it become interesting to break expectation and consider whether a new kind of closure is possible. In addition, I think there's also an issue about the self and ego of the artist. In Western literature, the ending to the *Divine Comedy* is an immense form of closure. It's thrilling to get to the end of the journey and experience "the love which moves the sun and the other stars." All of the cosmos is put into place, and Dante has supreme confidence in himself; but when the self is fractured and decentered, as it is, it's, again, virtually impossible to attain completion, and completion itself may not even be a goal.

DB: Section five is an even more concrete section. Emerson again: we have here a "bare list" of Native American tribes. Names like a roll call. This is the center section of the poem, midpoint. I know about your years of teaching at the Institute of American Indian Arts in Santa Fe. Are these tribes a representation of some of your past students' backgrounds? What's the desired effect here?

AS: I wrote "Spectral Line" during my last year of teaching at the Institute of American Indian Arts, and section five is indeed a roll call. At graduation each year, it is customary for students to be called on stage to receive their diploma, and their tribal affiliations follow their names. During the twenty-two years I taught at IAIA, I worked with students from, probably, two hundred tribes across the United States. Looking back, I thought of students who stood out, and, instead of their names, I used their tribes.

Many sections in "Spectral Line" leap and move with restless energy, but, at the center of this poem, I wanted to stop making large leaps and create some relative stillness. As the names of tribes are articulated, I wanted the naming to foreground the texture of sounds and for everything else to drop away. From an epistemological point of view, the roll call embodies the one and the many. All of the names are names of Native American tribes, yet, within that one, there's infinite variety.

DB: There is so much searching and hunting in the poem. For mushrooms, for names, for lovers, for knowledge, for meaningful ritual. And yet the poem also asserts that "nothing was at the center." That feels like the poem's truest discovery. Pieces, stories, the vulgar and the sublime together, and yet we don't find a center or a meaning so much as we find, well, the going-on of things—the provisional again—and the poem is about that going-on-ness, an acceptance of it. Is that a reasonable reading?

AS: Yes, though I think "nothing was at the center" may be misconstrued. From a Western perspective, "nothing" may appear to be a blank and feel disappointing; but from an Eastern perspective, there's a charged poetics of emptiness. For instance, here's a rough paraphrase of Chapter 11, from the *Dao De Jing*: "thirty spokes converge upon a single hub, but it is the hole in the center that enables the wheel and cart to move. You make a bowl from clay, but the empty space makes it useful. You make doors and windows for a room, but the empty space makes it livable. While the tangible has advantages, it is emptiness that makes it useful." In this light, the "nothing at the center" is thrilling and is the beginning of all creative possibility.

To come back to "Spectral Line," in section eight, when the speaker discovers the "nothing" at the center of things, he is discovering the source of all creation. In Stevens's world, it's where the imagination finds "what will suffice." In Yeats's world, it's where he writes, "Come near, come near, come near—Ah, leave me still / A little space for the rose-breath to fill!"

DB: That's wonderful—the positive aesthetic of the nothing. Silence as the perfect poetic.

Let me turn back further now to some of your earlier work. In 2003 we published your poem "Didyma." It's another poem that I think is central in your work. After its appearance in *KR*, you included it in your 2005 book *Quipu*.

You explain in a note to this book that quipus are textiles, and are found in old Asian as well as Incan cultures. They are a series of knotted cords used to keep records and make calculations and maybe tell stories. They are dyed strings, and they are "read" by the hands as well as eyes, is that right? They seem to me essentially a form of memory.

AS: I hesitate to call quipus textiles, because textiles usually implies woven fiber or fiber used in weaving. Merriam-Webster's defines a quipu as "a device made of a main cord with smaller varicolored cords attached and knotted and used by the ancient Peruvians (as for calculating)."

They are indeed a series of dyed, knotted cords, and it's important to distinguish numerical from non-numerical quipus. Numerical quipus employ different kinds of knots that encode the numbers one through nine, and the knots are placed at positions following a base-ten system. So numerical quipus are recording devices: They might show the amount of potatoes, even the kinds of potatoes, in storage, which would be crucial information during a famine. Non-numerical quipus, however, are believed to encode language. There's a historical account of an Inca runner who arrives at a village and, after he holds up the quipu, the indigenous people join a revolt against the Spanish. That account supports the thesis that quipus can also convey narrative information. In either case, the strings are "read" by the hands as well as eyes, and memory is an important factor.

DB: The quipu provides a useful analog for your poems. Tactile as well as textual, sensual, primitive, and again, possessed of a kind of equivalent representative system. Quipus are metaphors that don't make preferences as much as they make connections. And your poems connect things like science and ritual, the personal and the political, the organic and the synthetic; and, of course, your poems cross-reference so many cultures. Asian and Native American and Western and contemporary and ancient. Do you think of your poems, especially these longer sequences, as quipus?

AS: I conceived of the book *Quipu* (2005) as one large quipu, and the title poem, "Quipu," as one extended sequence inside of the larger one. In that book, I thought of language as fiber and deliberately worked with different forms of knotting. For instance, the repetitions of knotting can be seen in anaphora and epiphora. In the title poem, I used the word "as" many times but employed the dictionary's eleven different meanings so that the repetitions are elegant variations and layer the poem; but I don't think of my other sequences as quipus. Instead, they use a great variety of other structures or models.

DB: What are some of the other primary models for your poetry?

AS: I've used a variety of structures for my sequences. "Archipelago" braids the experience of a Zen garden with a Native American ceremony; "The String Diamond" utilizes the structure of go; "Earthshine" utilizes astronomy; "Six Persimmons" is an ekphrastic and is inspired by the eponymous painting; "Before Completion" draws on the divination text, the I Ching (Yijing).

   I've also created my own models. After I wrote many sectional sequences, Carol suggested that I try to write a sustained poem with a different model. I decided to open up the tercet form into a 1-2-2-1 form with indeterminate length. This model felt appropriate as a meditative space, and I created several poems using that form.

DB: Let's talk more about the poem. Didyma is an ancient Greek temple, though its location is in present-day Turkey. It ranked just below Delphi as the most important oracle sanctuary in the Hellenic world. So here you are working with another cultural narrative and tracing the structures of memory and vision.

Like "Spectral Line," your poem "Didyma" is a sectional poem. Some of the sections are tight, with rather linear narratives, while some are splayed with voices, pieces, tidbits, the found as well as the made. There's another wanderer here, a searcher, in part one, and in parts two and four we hear again the interplay of voices and images—pieces of disparate scenes—connected with semicolons. It's tempting to hear one voice as commenting on the previous, but it's also tempting to see the pieces are interchangeable and movable.

Was this poem written in a manner similar to "Spectral Line?"

AS: There are some similarities, but there are also important differences. Both sequences are grounded in a specific place, but, at Didyma, I experienced a crucial moment, which is part of its architectural design. Before reaching the inner sanctum, Carol and I walked down a dark and narrow vaulted ramp. The passage is long enough that your eyes adjust to the dark, but then you step out into sunlight and are literally dazzled. That intensely physical moment was also, for me, the experience of love, and I wrote that section first. From the compositional order, sections 8, 3, 4, 2, 1, 5, 6, 7, 9, 10, you can see that I had the end just before the expansive ending right at the outset. In "Spectral Line," however, I started with segments, section 4, and tried to create a microcosm or small signature of bands inside of what I knew would eventually be a much larger poem.

DB: The center of the poem, part five, comments on its own procedure: "A point of exhaustion can become a point of renewal." At this point the poem pauses, then opens into a more personal narrative. Your daughter appears, and the poem's location is clarified: a family trip to the Dardanelles and Black Sea—that is, a contemporary scene near the temple of Didyma. And so once more your poem becomes a series of layers, like a palimpsest. A thickly textured and richly historied scene. A mural. Section seven remains one of my favorite pieces of all your poems. It is a chant as much as a poem. I remember hearing you read "Didyma" years ago, and this section still haunts me. As you read it, you seemed to measure the time with your hands. Each segment was weighted and balanced, with the same amount of time as the others, and that wonderfully strange phrase—"it leopards the body"—served as a kind of rhythmic refrain. It is a sort of inverted cretic, by the way, to recall an old Greek meter in this new Greek narrative.

AS: I didn't know the Greek meter and am learning about it here from you. That's great.

DB: Well, I asked a classicist friend about this. That rhythm, "short long short / short long short," isn't a normative Greek meter, though just about every other triple-syllable foot is. He called it an inverted cretic, since a cretic is "long short long." Yours reverses that cadence.

AS: As a prelude to discussing the refrain, I want to say that in *Quipu* I consciously twisted nouns into verbs as part of the destabilization process. In the title poem, "Quipu," grief twists the language and turns nouns into verbs, "Loss salamanders the body, lagoons the mind." Later, there's "Did the knots of her loves jaguar in an instant?" So these unexpected twists help set up the refrain, "it leopards the body." In that section, I have white space before and after the refrain to give gravitas to it.

DB: In that phrase, what does "it" refer to? And "leopards" makes a wonderful verb—something spotted, pied, something that marks the body, or hunts it, or all of the above. How did you find that word?

AS: "It leopards the body" is used nine times in section seven. Here's the passage with the first occurrence:

"Do-as-you're-told scum sucker, you're the reason there are hydrogen bombs,"
yelled at the postal worker
behind the counter—

it leopards the body—

I thought the "it" might refer to the act of yelling which stains or spots the body. As each incident and refrain occurs, the "it" could refer to the preceding action, but it could also refer to a cumulative force from the world of experience. And, yes, I hoped "leopards" would mark and stain the body and make it hunted. My friend Rikki Ducornet once read a piece of fiction that used tiger as a verb, and I knew that someday I wanted to take another creature and turn it into a verb.

DB: The ultimate achievement of "Didyma" comes in sections nine and ten. Nine reads as a series of dependent clauses, commencing with a causal adverb "because." Section ten is, mostly, a series of independent clauses. But these sections appear on facing pages in your book, too, and this format invites us to read across the pages, across the spine, so that the clauses in nine are completed by those in ten. Thus: "Because one stirred the entrails of a goat immolated on an altar," // "nine purple irises bloom in a triangular glass vase," and so on.

That's just magnificent. The poem reads down the page, across the pages, and the effect is again to pluralize the possibilities. You make meaning out of the provisional, the accidental or random; and the coincidences of syntax and image created by the two sections becomes an additional layer of meaning. At least that's how I read these sections. Does that comply with your sense of it all?

AS: Absolutely. The reader is indeed invited to read across the pages and connect the first phrase in section nine beginning with "because" with the first phrase in section ten, as you just did.

Yet the possibilities become even more pluralized as a reader moves through the sections. For instance, in the second set of phrases, a reader encounters "because a magpie flicks tail feathers," and then, across the page, "a pearl forms in an oyster." Can this "because" phrase actually cause the pearl to form in an oyster?

The situation becomes more complex when you look at the thirteenth phrase, "because a grain of sand lodged," and notice that it aligns with the pearl forming in an oyster. A reader is then invited to explore the relationship between causes and effects diagonally across the pages. Ultimately, because the connections don't fit in any linear way, the two sections enact a suspension of all cause and effect, or enact universal cause and effect, and a reader bathes in the totality of experience. As such, it's a fitting end to "Didyma" and to the book.

DB: All along, then, Arthur, you have been working on poetry that gives us multiple choices, layers, alternatives. Many cultures, many ways of composing, many techniques of reading, and so on.

I imagine that your twenty-two years of teaching at IAIA involved a daily juggling of multi-cultural things. Do you think your teaching there affected your poetry so directly?

AS: In my early years of teaching, the Institute seethed with tensions and rivalries between different Native tribes, and I found it quite a challenge. I wasn't just juggling multi-cultural perspectives in class discussion. I often had to work with individual students to overcome cultural barriers and personal animosities.

At that stage, I resisted writing about my Native students, but over time, I found that my daily multi-cultural interactions had a growing and significant impact. In addition, I created a course, "The Poetic Image," where I showed Native students Tang dynasty Chinese poems. As I went through the poems character by character and showed students a variety of translations in English—some students then translated the poems into Native languages—it was inevitable that discussions about poetry, language, and culture sometimes clarified my own aesthetic positions and obliquely influenced my poetry.

DB: It's a very small school, as I recall, with something like two hundred and fifty students in all undergraduate degree programs. But many tribes are represented, from Inupiat in northern Alaska to Cherokee in Oklahoma. Were there common issues among the students? What kinds of special gifts—if any—did they possess as a characteristic of their backgrounds?

AS: The students often struggled with their ability to use English, but they always had a singular vitality along with a remarkable depth and diversity of lived experiences. They had a hunger and eagerness to experiment imaginatively, and those were two of their greatest strengths. In their creative writing, students were also eager to break stereotypical expectations.

DB: Do you still visit the campus?

AS: I became the first professor emeritus at the Institute in 2006, and I left with the understanding that I would keep in touch and return periodically. Each year I've returned during the fall semester to conduct a three-day residency that includes a reading, visits to poetry workshops, as well as individual conferences with creative writing majors.

DB: Are the students at IAIA inclined toward any particular kinds of poetry or particular treatments of material? More widely, what kinds of poetry do you see being written by the young these days across the country? What are their talents and what may be the challenges of the generation just emerging?

AS: The Institute students have always been willing to experiment with their writing, and their aesthetics are diverse. And that divergence, I think, is a strength in the kinds of poetry written by younger poets across the country. It's hard for me to articulate the challenges of the emerging generation—I'm confident they will do that for themselves.

DB: What are you reading these days that excites you? Are there any movements in contemporary poetry that you find notably discouraging and/or encouraging?

AS: I'm currently reading and excited by Dennis Tedlock's *Two Thousand Years of Mayan Literature* from the University of California Press. Although I'm interested in the loosely defined movement of ecopoetry, I don't want to privilege one group or movement over another. I certainly don't see myself as belonging to a movement or group, and I'd rather advocate a diversity of aesthetics. We live in a time where the complexities of our planet require a diverse array of compelling imaginative poetry. We need great poetry now more than ever before.

DB: How do you see your own poetry evolving in the near future? What are you working on, or what do you hope to work on?

AS: After completing *The Ginkgo Light* (2009), I've written a number of new poems, including the two short ones you published in the latest issue of *The Kenyon Review*. I recently met with Susan York, a sculptor and visual artist whose work I admire, and we decided to start a collaboration. Susan's drawings appear to be minimalist—she's currently working on a series of graphite drawings where the horizon line tilts ever so slightly from drawing to drawing—but the ultimate effects are large. Back in 1989 I collaborated with Tan Dun, and we created an ensemble work that combined poetry and music, but I've never collaborated with a visual artist before.

It will be interesting to see what happens.

II · BALANCING RIGOR AND SPONTANEITY

CHICAGO REVIEW INTERVIEW WITH ARTHUR SZE,
by Eric P. Elshtain (2004-05)

ERIC ELSHTAIN: Your books contain many long serial poems. What does writing a poetic sequence afford you—other than breadth and wider possibility—that you cannot achieve with a non-sequential short or long poem?

ARTHUR SZE: I believe the poetic sequence is the form of our time—mutable, capable of shifting voice as well as location, open to a variety of rhythms and structures. I have been drawn to the poetic sequence because it enables me to develop a complexity that intensifies as well as enlarges the scope and resonance of a poem. The word "complexity" is etymologically derived from "braiding together": I like to braid lyric, dramatic, and narrative elements and utilize them simultaneously. In writing a sequence—in contrast to a non-sequential short or long poem—I can make juxtaposition a more active structural principle. Because there are gaps—and here I think of the spaces as charged points of transformation—the point of focus can shift dramatically from one section to another. Within a single line, there can be juxtaposition between image and image; there can be juxtaposition between lines; and there can be juxtaposition between sections. When one section is juxtaposed to another section, a larger and deeper interaction takes place.

To make this clear, it might be helpful to look at the last two sections of my poem "Archipelago." One of the threads running through this sequence is a Pueblo ceremony: near the end of a social dance, there is often a "throw," where dancers throw objects (such as candy, cassette tapes, paper towels, etc.) out into the audience. The audience collects these objects, connects with the dancers, and thereby completes the ceremony. To complete the poem, and also the book, I designed a series of images that would be a "throw" to the reader. Section seven, which is block-like, ends with:

> The dancers reappear and enter the plaza in two lines.
> Shifting feet in rhythm to the shifting drumming,
> they approach the crowd under the yellow cottonwood.

And section eight begins:

> Mating above the cattails, red dragonflies—
>
> sipping lychee tea, eating fried scallion pancakes—
>
> bamboo slivers under the fingernails—

And it ends with:

> dancers are throwing
> licorice, sunflower seeds, pot scrubbers, aprons, plastic bowls.

Between the end of section seven and the beginning of section eight, I wanted to dissolve any literal connection between the dancers and the objects they throw. The space between sections is thus pivotal in that it releases the "throw" of images from a literal context. In this figurative "throw," I am intensifying the focus onto each line, where the white spaces are active.

In the employment of juxtaposition, I sometimes use it within a single line: for instance, in section nine, "black, *blak, blaec*" is the name for the work "black" in contemporary English, Middle English, and Old English. The words are hom-onyms—they all sound the same—yet the spelling shifts so that the attention is turned from present toward the past. That perspective helps set up the follow-ing two lines: "following the thread / of recollection through a lifetime—". This two-line stanza is then juxtaposed with, "the passions becoming the chiming sounds of jade." I hope each of these lines has a clarity and energy reminiscent of Japanese haiku, but their juxtapositions create a unique complex.

If you look at the last line of section eight, and the opening line to section nine, "Plastic bowls, aprons, pot scrubbers, sunflower seeds, licorice," you will see that the list (a catalogue within a single line) is reversed. In the first naming, it is as if dancers threw out the list of objects, but, in the second naming, the motion is reversed: it is as if the action is going backward or is being erased. Because I am trying to heighten the experience of transience in the phenomenal world, I try to endow each line with this resonance and end with, "egrets wading in shal-low water at low tide."

EE: Do you throw the *I Ching*? If so, what relationship do you see between predicated divination systems and the writing of poetry? Also, do you use yarrow? Coins?

AS: Divination can mean "the art or practice that seeks to foresee or foretell future events or discover hidden knowledge," and I'm interested in the latter.

Poetry can have an epistemological slant, and I like poetry that incorporates some of the functions of philosophy: for instance, how do we come to know truths about ourselves and the world?

Although I had been interested in the *I Ching* for many years, I first consulted it in 1994. Naomi Shihab Nye called me early one morning to say she had just heard that the exiled Chinese poet, Gu Cheng, had killed his wife and hanged himself in New Zealand. I was shaken and distressed by the news. I sat down and threw coins six times and generated the very last hexagram, "Before Completion." When I read the oracle response, I wondered if the title referred to Gu Cheng as a poet who died before he had a chance to complete his life's work. In considering the pattern of broken and solid lines, I realized I might be able to write a sequence that employed fragmentary as well as block-like sections, where the broken sections possessed yin energy and the solid sections possessed yang energy. I also thought an intermediary form might be equivalent to a changing line. As I worked for months on this sequence, I shed the literal connection to the order of solid and broken lines that compose this hexagram, but I retained the title.

Since 1994 I have consulted the *I Ching* many times. I usually employ the coin method: it is quick, and it has been said that the coin method is appropriate for the quick pace of our world. On several occasions, I have used the yarrow method with my wife, Carol Moldaw, and we have generated hexagrams together. The yarrow method is much slower: for instance, at the outset, one gathers the fifty stalks and sets one aside to represent the infinite. The tactile, shifting procedure has more suspense; yet, in either procedure, the element of chance is physically manifest.

Although I admire the *I Ching* for its synchronicity, its archetypal visualization of states of transformation, I'm ultimately using it as a source of inspiration for my own poetry. I recently wanted to write an extended poem without sections and I consulted the *I Ching* on several occasions. As I read commentaries for various hexagrams, I decided to invent a form that utilized odd and even numbers (1-2-2-1 etc.) that could extend for an indefinite length. The result is a new poem, "The Angle of Reflections Equals the Angle of Incidence."

EE: The title "Before Completion" leads me to the question: Do you feel that your poems capture a moment of ordering phenomena, or are they a refinement of that order? Can you identify an ordering principle behind your poems, even if it changes as the poem comes to an end?

AS: I like to recall Stevens's dictum to find and not impose. In my sequences, I usually have a loose structural principle that helps me order the motion, but I usually have to write a series of sections before I can find what the appropriate structure might be. In "The String Diamond," for instance, I wrote several sections before I discerned that a viable structure might be the ancient Chinese board game, *wei ch'i*, which is better known in America by its Japanese name, *go*. After I discovered this structure, I was able to pursue some of its implications. For instance, I wrote section three, which is a catalog of endangered species, with the idea that it was equivalent to placing one stone directly linked to another stone directly linked to another (which, in the course of the game, is a sure way to lose). I don't expect a reader to identify these underlying structures, but I hope that a reader feels an inner necessity.

EE: You say that you "hope the reader feels an inner necessity" and that "disorientation may be a necessary early stage in a reader's experience of the poem." You also say that the poem "The String Diamond" has a structure based on the board game wei ch'i. What moves do readers have to make when they read your poetry or any other poetry for that matter? What's your sense of how a reader "finishes" any given poem he/she reads? Why is focus so important as a final experience of the poem?

AS: When I say that I hope a reader feels an inner necessity, I mean that when a reader reads a poem of mine—or anyone's poem for that matter—I hope that reader feels an underlying rigor, a visceral recognition that the words need to be in the order they're in to make a poem happen. When a poem does not rely on overt narrative as a structure, a reader may become initially disoriented because there is no easy connection or causation. These moments of disorientation, however, may be extremely helpful and may resemble koans that stretch the mind. Traditional narrative tends to move in a single space-time, but what happens if there are multiple space-times inside a single poem? This is what the structure of that boardgame allowed me. An understanding of specific moves and rules of *go*, or *wei ch'i*, is not a prerequisite—such knowledge might actually be an impediment—but I do ask a reader to be attentive and be willing to stretch.

I think endings to poems are important. I agree with Emily Dickinson, who once wrote, "A word is dead / When it is said, / Some say. // I say it just / Begins to live / That day." I like endings to have a combination of finesse and strength, so that the poem begins to grow in the reader's body and mind just as the words end. Over time, I have consciously explored a variety of endings. Here are four examples: in "The Silk Road," the poem ends with language and naming, "as now I say *now*"; in "Archipelago," it ends with an image, "egrets wadding in shallow water at low tide"; in "Six Persimmons," it ends with a metaphor, "their fingertips glow in the skin of their days"; in "Kaiseki," it ends with an assertion, "water flows to what is wet."

EE: I want to ask something about the Native American inflections in your work, but am having trouble formulating a question that doesn't seem pedantic or even insulting on a certain level. You work at a Native American school, and your poems often mention objects and ritual from different tribal traditions. Do you see these as counter-traditions, in the way that Pound felt about Chinese thought and belief? Are they antidotes to the usual way we see and communicate?

AS: I have taught at the Institute of American Indian Arts in Santa Fe for seventeen years. At any given time, Native students from over a hundred tribes across the United States come to study creative writing, museum studies, two-dimensional or three-dimensional arts. The Institute has a four-year BFA degree program as well as a two-year AA degree. In the time that I've been at the Institute, I've probably worked with students from at least two hundred tribes, and they are all ages. eighteen to eighty.

I don't see these Native traditions as counter-traditions in the way that Pound felt about Chinese thought and belief. I think for Pound, classic Chinese poetry came as a shock and revelation, and he used those thoughts and beliefs as a counter tradition to the Western European tradition. In my case, I'm more interested in ideas of multiplicity. In working with students who are, say, Inuit, Mohawk, Navajo, Tsalagi, Pueblo, I'm often learning a variety of cultural perspectives and am constantly challenged. From 1978 to 1995, I was also married to a Hopi weaver (our son is Chinese and Hopi), so Native experiences were part of my everyday life. Without initially intending to use Native traditions, they have become a deep and enriching influence on my work.

EE: In your translations of Chinese poetry, you're working with visually based characters which, if I'm correct, cannot really be distinguished prepositionally or differentiated between singulars and plurals. How do you deal with the radical differences between the Chinese ideogram and the alphabetically and phonetically based English?

AS: In the introduction to *The Silk Dragon* (Copper Canyon, 2001), I mention that translation is an impossible task, and that as a translator I am aware of loss and transformation, destruction and renewal. Chinese and English are radically different languages. One of the first losses is in the sound: Chinese is a tonal language, and it is impossible to carry those effects over. To be concrete, it may be instructive to look at Ma Chih-yuan's "Autumn Thoughts," a classic poem from the Yuan dynasty:

枯　藤　老　樹　昏　鴉

小　橋　流　水　人　家

古　道　西　風　瘦　馬

夕　陽　西　下

斷　腸　人　在　天　涯

In the original Chinese, as you can see, there are five lines: lines one, two, three, and five have six characters each, but line four has only four characters. As you mention, a Chinese character does not, in itself, differentiate between singular and plural, yet this ambiguity is used to virtuoso effect. If I approximate the Chinese characters and use a word in English for each Chinese character, the shape for the first three lines is:

dry	vine/s	old	tree/s	dusk	crow/s
small	bridge/s	flow	water/s	man/men	house/s
ancient	road/s	west	wind	lean	horse/s

The poem proceeds by suspending two characters at a time across the line. Are the nouns singular or plural: which ones are singular, which ones plural? Where is the vine in relation to the tree? Where is the crow, or where are the crows in relation to the vines and trees? Are the crows flying in the sky? Or are they perched on branches of old trees? In this landscape, where is the small bridge? Are there several bridges that cross a single stream that winds back and forth? Or are there several streams in the landscape? And where is man? Are there a few men in the landscape? Where are they in relation to the houses? Is there one ancient road? Or are there several? Although we get the presence of the west wind, what does that signify? The character for "road" is also the word for "Tao," the way. Is there one lean horse or several lean horses, and where are they? Should you, as a reader, notice that the character "lean," has the sickness radical?

To complete the poem, here are the last two lines:

| setting | sun | west | down | | |
| break | guts | man | at | sky's | edge |

In line four, the pattern of six characters to a line is broken; as a reader, it is important to feel that something is missing; the silence—where two more characters are expected but none are given—weights and tilts the poem. What is it for the sun to be going down? Is it worth noting that the character for sun, "yang" is also yang energy, light, the male principle, descending down to darkness. In the last line, the character for man seems to denote a single man. It would be silly to have a bunch of men lined up along the horizon, at the sky's edge. Instead, it makes sense for there to be one miniscule man.

If you look at the title, "Autumn Thoughts," the character autumn has tree tips on fire. Juxtaposition becomes a form of metaphor: autumn = tree tips + fire. When you look at thoughts, the character has an above and below: field above and heart/mind below. The metaphor here is: to think is to put your heart in a field: thought = heart/mind + field. The form of this poem is a *chü*, usually translated as a song. Although this poem does not occur inside a play, it is important to remember that Ma Chih-yuan, author of "Autumn in the Palace of Han," is also a great playwright. It is tempting to read this poem as a miniature soliloquy: there may be a hint that as the sun goes down, so does the yang energy, and, with it, the dynasty.

You can see how so many of the discussed elements defy translation. I've tried to keep the English spare so that a reader can get close to the motion in the original Chinese. I normally like to write out a cluster of words in English under each Chinese word to help demarcate its field of energy. In this case, I've kept the English minimal, so that a reader can experience how the poem unfolds in a scroll-like fashion. When I made a translation of this poem into English, I wanted to use short lines to indicate this slow, unfolding motion. I used three lines in English for each line of Chinese, except for line four, where I broke the symmetry of the three-line stanzas to mark the shift or break in the Chinese.

AUTUMN THOUGHTS

Withered vine,
old tree,
crows.

A small bridge,
flowing water,
houses.

Ancient road,
west wind,
lean horse.

Sun sinking
in the west—

and a man,
crushed,
at the sky's edge.

EE: You talk about spaces as "charged points of transformation" and "active" and that it is "important to feel that something is missing." How do these spaces act on the mind? How is a reader meant to "read" space in the midst of a poem?

AS: When Ma Chih-yuan sets out the first three lines with six characters to a line, he sets up an expectation for that form to continue. When line four has only four characters, the established pattern is broken, and it creates a pivotal moment. Because there is an empty space where two characters are expected, a reader is invited to speculate on what might go in the space. The space, or silence, thus pivots the poem so that what follows is given special attention. In "Autumn Thoughts," the breaking of the symmetry applies a special pressure and focus onto the "man, crushed, at the sky's edge."

In regard to larger issues in poetics, I believe many contemporary poets do not utilize silences, or white spaces, to their full capacity in their poems. White spaces on the page help demarcate where and how long the silences are, and, as a counterpoint to sound, silences are an essential part of the poem. In this sense, the white spaces are "active." Like yin energy that contains a yang dot, these silences can also be "charged points of transformation," where they help charge the language that is there.

As a final comment, an analogy with Asian calligraphy might be instructive. Initially, one wants to draw the characters in black ink according to their specific stroke order and direction, but, as one progresses, one is instructed to no longer paint the black, but rather, paint the white. This is perhaps a more profound way of conceiving of the white spaces in a poem.

EE: You once mentioned to me that you held up the publication of your new and selected poems, *The Redshifting Web,* until you finished your amazing poem, "Six Persimmons." Why was that poem so important to include in your collected poems?

AS: I wanted to open *The Redshifting Web* with some of my best work and felt challenged to do something different. I wanted to write a poem that did not openly rely on fragmentation, that repeated its form, yet transformed itself from the inside out. For a long time I've admired the classic Ch'an painting, "Six Persimmons," and, as I considered it, I had the idea that a sequence could delineate, at six different stages, a parabolic curve of ripening. The spaces between the sections did not need to demarcate equally spaced moments of ripening; rather, there could be a motion from opacity toward transparency where the ripening effect accelerated through the sections. I don't think I could have articulated any of this while I was composing the poem, but, in hindsight, I had a loose structure that could modify as I went along. When I completed "Six Persimmons," I felt it was a cornerstone to the new work.

EE: Is poetry something like a biology of the human mind? A kind of hallucinogen, perhaps, for the reader?

AS: I am interested in altered and altering states of mind. Disorientation should not be the final response to a poem, but disorientation may be a necessary early stage in a reader's experience of a poem. In order to re-envision the world, the eventual focus needs to be earned. Because poems are intense experiences, I like poems that present a heightened or intensified form of being and becoming.

EE: Is a poem a heuristic device for the mind to use to interact with the transient phenomenal world?

AS: Rilke once said that discussions about poems end up more or less as misunderstandings, so I hesitate here. I don't like to think of poems as heuristic: "involving or serving as an aid to learning, discovery, or problem-solving by experimental and esp. trial-and-error methods." It's possible one can write a poem with such ideas in mind (*The Divine Comedy* might have started out this way, but doesn't it become something else in the end?), but it's probably too programmatic.

In the case of some poems that refer to divination and are focused on the transient phenomenal world, such as "Before Completion" or "The String Diamond," all I can say is that I was interested in exploring chance and fate, fragility, mutability, but was interested in the possibility of some larger, archetypal structure that might underlie these exploration. I think Picasso once said that when starting a work of art it's good to have an idea in mind, but that it always becomes something else in the end.

EE: The "archetypal structure" you mention raises a question about metaphor. In your earlier work, especially in *Dazzled* (Floating Island, 1982)—which seems to be a state of mind—metaphoric formulae are more explicit; the present indicative "is" is used over and over again to build a web of associations and metamorphoses. This formula all but disappears in your later work. Does this change have to do with a shift in your understanding of poetry, or of the natural world, or both?

AS: As you say in *Dazzled*, I often make metaphor explicit: x is y, "The Moon is a Diamond." That kind of explicit statement is still present in *River River* (Lost Roads, 1987)—the opening poem is titled, "The Leaves of a Dream Are the Leaves of an Onion,"—but I think it begins to dissolve in that book. By the time of *Archipelago* (Copper Canyon, 1995), this kind of metaphorical assertion has vanished. I became more interested in metaphor that has the linguistic shape of x juxtaposed to y (as in "The Redshifting Web") or x(y) (as in "Archipelago"), where the completion of the metaphor is not explicit.

In the course of the evolution, my own conception of poetry shifted. I like to relate an anecdote from Japanese tea ceremony: a merchant once purchased an expensive bowl and invited Sen no Rikyu to conduct tea ceremony. The merchant hoped to impress Rikyu with this artifact, but when the merchant asked how Rikyu liked it, he showed no particular interest and went on his way. The merchant was so angry he took the bowl, threw it on the floor, and shattered it into pieces. When a servant came in to sweep up the pieces, he decided to collect the shards and glued them back together. One day Rikyu came back, and when he saw that irregular tea bowl, he exclaimed," What a fantastic bowl; who made it?"

In many ways, my early poems were like artifacts: I admired the traditional compression and clarity of classical Chinese poetry, and I liked poems that could be accomplished in, say, twenty to thirty lines. But I realized that these poems were too much like artifacts and that the mind was too much in control. I also wanted to bring more of the world into the poem, and I like how in the parable of the tea story, emotion shatters the well-made vessel and breaks it apart so that it can be transformed and made new. In many ways I was searching for ways to shatter my own conception of a poem, and my understanding of the world was also deepening. I was searching for a poem that could enact an imaginative balance between rigor and spontaneity.

An Interview with Arthur Sze, by Tony Leuzzi (2012)

TONY LEUZZI: At the end of your poem, "The Living Room," you write, "I close / my eyes, feel how in the circumference / of a circle the beginning and end have no end." Similarly, the ending of the sixth section of "Inflorescence" also refers to circles: "And what appears to be up close a line / becomes by air, the arc of a circle." These are just two among many instances in your poems where references to circles emerge. Moreover, many of your poems are circular in form, insofar as they begin with some image or phrasing that is echoed in the final lines. Can you discuss the importance of circles in your work?

ARTHUR SZE: Geometries of space—point, line, web, and circle—are significant motifs in my work. I'd like to start by quoting from Emerson's essay, "Circles," in which he asserts, "Around every circle another circle can be drawn." Each circle implies a series of ever-expanding concentric circles and is an image of the expanding cosmos. Emerson also asserts circles are "the highest emblem of the cipher of the world." Here I'm more interested in "cipher" than in the hierarchy of "the highest emblem," and I read "cipher" as zero, emptiness, and mystery. From an Eastern perspective, the *enso*, or Zen circle, can represent void, totality, or even enlightenment. If you inscribe Emerson's beliefs in one circle, and Zen beliefs in another, as in a Venn diagram, they overlap extensively; and the circle of my beliefs would overlap with both.

Two examples from my work might be helpful. First, at the end of "Streamers," I mention a circle as "a dot that must enlarge into / a zero: a void, *enso*, red shimmer, / breath, endless beginning, pure body, pure mind." In many poems, I play with scale, and here the circle appears, at a distance, to be a period, to put finality and closure on things; but, if you look up close, what appears to be a period may actually be a circle that contains emptiness. The dot, then, is a circle that incorporates red shimmer, breath, endless beginning, pure body, pure mind; so the circle is not a static one-dimensional symbol but rather, emptiness rich in possibility, a three-dimensional force actualized in breathing.

I want to add that circularity often involves returning to see or experience something again for the first time, and it doesn't have to enact closure. "Because a circle opens in all directions," it enables connections to form in an infinite array. Point, line, spiral, web, and circle all connect. In a second example, "Labrador Tea," I begin with the image of "labrador leaves in a jar with a kerchief lid." The poem moves through a series of associations and comes back at the end to "leaves clothed underneath with rusty hairs / suffuse a boreal light glistening on tidal pools." I cite this poem, because the circling motion does not enact formal closure. Instead, when the return takes place, I hope the reader discovers that the poem occurs during the time that labrador leaves have been steeping—the tea is now ready to drink!

TL: In an outstanding interview you did with Eric P. Elshtain for *Chicago Review*, you state: "I believe the poetic sequence is the form of our time . . . I have been drawn to the poetic sequence because it enables me to develop a complexity that intensifies as well as enlarges the scope and resonance of a poem." That interview was published in 2004 shortly before the publication *Quipu* (2005), which, though not mentioned there, features many poetic sequences. The same goes for *The Ginkgo Light* (2010). Although you explain your reasons for using the poetic sequence in that interview, I was wondering if you could discuss them again—a task that will require some repetition, of course, but, considering your persistent and extensive use of the form since then, some enlargement as well.

AS: I still believe the poetic sequence is the form of our time. In 2004, I mentioned several important factors: I could (a) "develop a complexity that intensifies as well as enlarges the scope and resonance of a poem," (b) "make juxtaposition a more active structural principle," and (c) "braid lyric, dramatic, and narrative elements and utilize them simultaneously." I continue to affirm these points but want to add that the enormous flexibility of the sequence is one of its greatest strengths. Unlike a narrative that relies on a fairly linear unfolding in time, with a sequence, I can more easily change location or character, shift focus and tone, vary rhythm, and radially amplify thematic concerns.

In writing sequences, I'm still very interested in exploring the relationship between part and whole, and my conception of fragmentation inside of sequences has shifted between the *Chicago Review* interview (2004-05) and today. In my sequences through 1998, I often conceived of fragments as shards of a pot. I liked the jagged edges and how the stillness between them suspended narrative motion. When I wrote *Quipu*, I began to conceive of fragments as carded but unspun fiber—in weaving, one cards or aligns fibers before spinning them into a one-ply yarn—where images and thematic concerns were visible and unharnessed. In *The Ginkgo Light,* I conceived of fragments more as line segments than uncarded fiber, and only occasionally as shards. In any case, when sequences incorporate fragments inside of a larger whole, they are not merely complex. A sequence is most cogent if it integrates the one and the many, so that it is complex and simple at the same time.

To give an example, I'd like to discuss "Spectral Line." After teaching for twenty-two years at the Institute of American Indian Arts, I wanted to write about some of my experiences there but found that a single narrative line wasn't capacious enough to respond to the complexity of cross-cultural tensions. The definition of a spectral line—on small scale, a particular wavelength of light corresponding to an energy transition—gave me the "one" which I could amplify into "many" manifestations. As I wrote, I found that, in addition to a loose narrative that harnesses incidents from the Institute, it was important to add a second narrative where a speaker journeys to China. I initially conceived of these two narrative strands as continual points of comparison and contrast. Then one day a third narrative unexpectedly entered the poem. A character, Robin, appears in the second line, where she adjusts the saddle on a horse. She disappears for much of the poem and then reappears in section seven, where a reader learns that she quit her job in the telecommunications industry after her coworkers were terminated, and now she grooms "the horses she loves." This is the barest of narratives, but it applies psychological pressure to the situation at hand. Robin's narrative radially amplifies the issue of how people treat each other, and, in writing a fluid sequence that wasn't tied to linear narration, I was able to let her enter, exit, and reenter without difficulty.

Finally, I want to add that I find the gaps between sections of a sequence supremely useful. A new section can start far from where the last section ended, create tension and surprise, though ultimately it has to connect and become part of the essential fabric.

TL: One of the most salient features of your poetry since *Dazzled* (1982) is its simultaneous accessibility and difficulty. On one hand, the poems do not pose too many linguistic challenges. There is, in fact, a disarmingly direct and unadorned simplicity of utterance. Many of your poems, for example, braid together a series of basic grammatical structures: "I gaze … I notice … you stare … they walk …" On the other hand, the poems require a considerable amount of intellectual rigor to be adequately understood, partially because of the subtlety of the juxtapositions, partially because you are grappling with complicated ideas, and partially because you dramatize complicated moments of perception. Can you talk about these tensions between accessibility and difficulty in your poems?

AS: As you say, the basic grammatical structures in my poems are often direct. In addition, I value clarity, and that gives my imagery and descriptive language broad accessibility. Yet I also employ a wide vocabulary, and many words from different disciplines—quipu, *omega minus*—and different languages—*dhyana*, *xun*—can be a hurdle. In addition, my syntax and sentences were simpler in my early work, but, as evidenced by the increasing use of semi-colons, dashes, and colons, they've become more nuanced. Juxtaposition is another difficulty for some readers, because rather than a linear narrative where B follows from A, A and B are placed into simultaneous interaction with each other without resolution.

Here I want to add that I am not writing to be difficult: I am writing the poems I need to write, and I'm keenly interested in creating polysemous poems. To accomplish that, depth and layering are important. I like to invoke the Japanese aesthetic term, *yugen*: the two characters have been translated as "subtle," "profound," "mysterious," and, in the words of a former Japanese student, "almost disappearing." The *yu* character is, in one etymology, derived from indigo dyeing. In that art, a dyer dips a skein of spun white silk into an indigo vat, soaks it, and pulls it up into the air. When indigo comes in contact with oxygen, it chemically reacts, and the yarn turns greenish-blue. After repeated dippings, the yarn changes in color from greenish-blue to blue to deep blue to blue-approaching-black. At this last stage, it arrives at that state of mystery, subtlety, and profundity.

I hope that the depth and multiplicity in my poems strike a reader immediately, even though he/she cannot immediately articulate what is happening. I also hope that initial shock leads to a vibrancy that impels a reader to come back again and again. In this process of engagement, I hope that some of the initial disorientation or difficulty that my poems cause are experienced as necessary steps or stages toward experiencing a new totality, and that, as the poems reveal themselves over time, this experience is enriching and compelling.

TL: You are a second-generation Chinese American who has strong geographical and cultural ties to the American Southwest—particularly New Mexico and the Native American tribes there. How have you absorbed both the Chinese and Native American traditions into your work?

AS: I have absorbed the Chinese literary and cultural tradition through translation and through my family. When I was a student at UC Berkeley, I approached Ts'ai Mei-hsi, an instructor in conversational Mandarin, after class, and showed him my translation of a Tang dynasty poem. I asked Ts'ai if he would respond to it, and he got excited and said he loved Tang poetry. He offered to meet me at the Oriental Languages library, and, there, he checked the accuracy of my translations and also looked up geographical and historical references. Our meetings were never part of a class, but, with his help, I translated twenty-nine poems by Li Bo, Du Fu, Wang Wei, and a few others. A decade later, I translated poems from other time periods, by such poets as Tao Qian, Li Qingzhao, Ma Zhiyuan, and Wen Yiduo, who broke from the classical tradition and wrote in the vernacular. A decade after, I translated a third set of poems and collected all of my translations in *The Silk Dragon* (2001).

I thought my work as a translator of Chinese poetry might be over, but then, from 2002-2008, I was invited to China, Taiwan, and Hong Kong for international poetry festivals and met many of the leading poets. I decided to translate a fourth set of poems by Xi Chuan, Chen Li, and Yang Lian. Then in 2009, Ed Hirsch invited me to edit *Chinese Writers on* Writing for the Trinity University Press *Writers on Writing* series. Instead of selecting writings from across two thousand years, I decided to focus on modern Chinese poetry and fiction. I selected all of the writings and, with the help of many translators, assembled a collection of essays by forty-one Chinese writers from 1917 to 2009. So, over time, my work as a translator and editor has enabled me to absorb a large part of the Chinese literary tradition.

In terms of cultural tradition, I've drawn extensively from my family background as well as travel in China. My parents were immigrants and spoke Mandarin and English at home. My father had, in his library, such classics as the *Lao-zi, Zhuang-zi*, and *Yi Jing*, and I remember, as a teen, puzzling over them. In 1985 I traveled for a month with an uncle in China and visited my mother's family's home outside Beijing and also sailed, before the dam was built, a thousand miles down the Yangtze River. My uncle introduced me to friends and relatives; he and an aunt were particularly interested in Chinese history, and I learned a lot from them.

I also have a long connection with Native American culture. After I graduated from UC Berkeley, I moved to Santa Fe and worked as a poet in the schools. I conducted workshops at a number of Indian pueblos and met Ramona Sakiestewa, a Hopi weaver, through the New Mexico Arts Division. We were married from 1978-1995, and our son, Micah, is an enrolled member of the Hopi tribe. During those years, I experienced the gritty as well as the sacred in contemporary Native life.

In addition, from 1984-2006, I was on the faculty at the Institute of American Indian Arts. During those years, I worked daily with students from over two hundred tribes across the United States and was privileged to teach and learn from them. Many of my former students have become writers, and they include Sherwin Bitsui, James Thomas Stevens, Allison Hedge Coke, Jennifer Foerster, Irvin Morris, Orlando White, Layli Long Soldier, Santee Frazier, DG Okpik, Cathy Rexford, Sara Ortiz, and Eddie Chuculate. Over time, my experiences at the Institute greatly widened and deepened my understanding of Native culture.

TL: Despite your many links to Chinese and Native American cultures, you are an American poet. How would you situate yourself in the tradition of American Poetry?

AS: My links with Chinese and Native American cultures are significant influences and sources of inspiration, but, yes, absolutely, I am an American poet. I hope it is not too presumptuous to invoke Whitman, Williams, Pound, and Stevens to say I am in conversation with them. With Whitman, I share an interest in the possibilities of the poetic sequence, an impulse to inventory and catalog and make a living record, and I share his inclusive vision and desire to put worlds inside of poetry. With Williams, I share "deep noticing," an interest in dispassionate presentation of the thing itself, and in harnessing luminous particulars. Ezra Pound's imagism drew on the primacy of the image in classical Chinese poetry and drove it deep into American modernism, and, with Pound, I share a keen interest in the poetic image, the use of juxtaposition as an active, structural principle, and the braiding of cultures. With Stevens, I share an abiding interest in the relationship between the mind/imagination and the world, a search for "what will suffice," and in meditative duration. I share his belief that "poetry must resist the intelligence almost successfully."

TL: Certain concepts—such as expansion and contraction, loss and retrieval, recollection and transformation—are revisited throughout your work. Certain images reemerge as well: acequias, arroyos, blood, mushrooms, candles, moons, gates, light. Never are these repetitions repetitious or merely repetitions. Instead, I see you writing, in the interests of clarity and rediscovery, the same poem again and again, inscribing your signature upon a constellation of themes in new and fresh ways. In this way, your work reminds me of Whitman's. Would you agree or disagree with this, and can you explain how it is true or not true for you?

AS: I'd like to begin by responding to the issue of repetitions. Anthropologists assert that repeating patterns and images are not mere repetitions but are "forms of insistence," and that these forms of insistence reveal the very fabric of a culture. In a similar way, my repeating images and patterns are variations that widen, deepen, and enrich the meanings of a poem. On a micro-level, in "Quipu," I use the word "as" twenty times, but I am utilizing different denotative meanings so that each time the word recurs, a new layer and resonance is added. Eventually this process is explicitly revealed when the poem asserts, "as: to the same degree or amount; / for instance; when considered in a specified // form or relation; in or to the same degree / in which; as if; in the way or manner that; // in accordance with what or the way in which; / while, when; regardless of the degree to which; // for the reason that; that the result is."

I'd also like to propose that the view that I am "writing, in the interests of clarity and rediscovery, the same poem again and again, inscribing [my] signature upon a constellation of themes in new and fresh ways" is a helpful point of departure but is ultimately limiting, because it doesn't fully allow for progression. Like Whitman, I am indeed interested in a constellation of themes, but my style, as well as thematic concerns, have shifted from book to book. From *Dazzled* (1982) to *River River* (1987), you can see a significant enlargement of scope and imaginative command. In *River River*, I wrote my first sequences, and there have been significant changes since then. *Archipelago* foregrounded part and whole, while *Quipu* foregrounded linguistic experimentation. Also, there's an erotic charge in the section of new poems in *The Redshifting Web* that carries over and informs *Quipu*. If I've shifted my scientific interest from physics in *River River* to living biology in *The Ginkgo Light*, from inquiries into the nature of the cosmos to considering the immediate challenges of our imperiled world, I believe this change is no longer about putting my signature upon a constellation of themes. Instead, the poems become landmarks on a journey.

Finally, I'd like to add that currently I'm collaborating with Susan York, an artist here in Santa Fe. After spending hours in her studio, discussing her graphite sculptures and drawings, and seeing how she incorporates a "record of labor" into her art, I've written a new sequence, "The Unfolding Center," in eleven sections. Sections three and eight are monologues in different voices, and, as the speakers talk, they revise what they say, and these passages are visually marked with strike-through lines. The two voice-driven sections create key points of tension with some of the more image-driven sections, and this creative tension is elevated and incorporated into the very fabric of the poem. I believe this is a new achievement, so the notion of writing the same poem again and again, or writing with a constellation of themes in mind is no longer adequate to describe the progression in my work.

TL: In a 1977 interview with Christopher Busa, Stanley Kunitz said, "The vocabulary of modern science is fascinating . . . but, by and large, [it] remains exclusive and specialized." Such terminology, he insisted, should be as common to us as myths were to the ancient Greeks. I mention this to you because your writing engages the language of science—be it physics, astronomy, botany, or other branches of science—more thoroughly and deeply than any poet I can think of. And your use of such terminology, though precise, is never dry or merely technical. It does what Kunitz felt the language of myth did for the ancient Greeks: it gave them a language with which to grapple with the mysteries of the world; it gave them a language—however imperfect—with which to make sense of space and one's place in it. How did you develop the richness of your scientific vocabulary and how do you see its place in your poems?

AS: I've mentioned in other interviews that I started to write poetry at MIT. I spent my first two years of college there and then transferred to UC Berkeley. During my freshman year, I took the usual courses in physics, calculus, and organic chemistry, but if my knowledge of science had stopped there, it would not have become very interesting. Years later in New Mexico, I met Dick Slansky, a physicist who became the director of the theoretical physics division at Los Alamos National Laboratory. Conversations with Dick sparked my interest in what physicists were working on, and he inevitably discussed string theory and other issues. Through him, I met other physicists, including George Zweig and Murray Gell-Mann, the Nobel laureate. Conversations with Dick, George, and Murray widened and deepened my understanding and helped me develop the richness of my vocabulary in science. From Murray, I learned about complexity theory, and, he, in turn, titled his book, *The Quark and the Jaguar*, after a phrase from one of my poems. In addition, over five summers, Micah and I took a mushroom identification class with naturalist Bill Isaacs, and we learned how to identify many species, as well as their habitats.

It's a delight to read your excerpt from Stanley Kunitz's 1977 interview, and I am in agreement with him. Although scientific languages are specialized, I find their vocabularies and structures helpful to talk about the world. Unlike scientists, I think of these terms as contemporary languages of myth. For instance, who knows if string theory will provide a breakthrough or be relegated to the dustbins of scientific history, but, for now, it's an engaging vision, and it gives us a vehicle with which to grapple with the mysteries of the cosmos. When I was writing *The Ginkgo Light*, I became fascinated by the biology of the ginkgo leaf: the initial vein bifurcates and each subsequent vein bifurcates so that, instead of a web, the veins branch endlessly. When I did further research and discovered that a ginkgo tree survived the atomic blast at Hiroshima and flowered a week later, I found an image of nature pushed to the brink, and also a mythic response. So scientific inquiry has informed, strengthened, and even inspired my poetry, but I do not feel bound by it.

I want to add that I like using the structures of science to give underlying rigor to the poem and in that sense they can help shape it. I don't want to hit a reader over the head with "look, here is science." I liken the scientific motif to a thread that appears and disappears, that reappears and disappears. By not calling attention to itself, a reader who doesn't know the science can still experience what is happening in the poem. I like poems that have mystery and surprise:

poems that you have to read and reread and that reveal themselves over time. I never want to feel like a reader has to have certain sets of knowledge to be able to appreciate the poem I am writing. I just want the reader to come to my poems with open eyes, to read with their nerves, so to speak, to be open to experience.

TL: Reading with their nerves, that is interesting…

AS: Reading a poem is a visceral experience. Emily Dickinson said, "I know it's a poem if it takes the top of my head off." I like that intense visceral reaction. And I use "nerves" because when I'm reading someone else's poem I might not know where I'm going or what's going to happen. I'm sensing with my nerves a multiplicity of effects in language; it's imaginative and it's emotional. That's why I proposed reading with one's nerves. It is not only intimate and vulnerable, but also electric and powerful.

TL: A poem that takes one's head off would more likely appear in a compressed poem, a single movement. Given the serial nature of your poems, and that you often write poems that are spread over pages, do you want the reader to have an "it takes my head off" reaction the whole way through, or do you feel there are moments of intensity that are followed by a certain slackening, and then intensification, and so forth?

AS: That's a wonderful question. If it's a compressed poem, I sometimes hope the reader has that experience at the end. But in a sequence, spread over many pages, I wouldn't want that to happen again and again; in fact if it did, if you repeatedly and deliberately try to startle or stun a reader, I believe it would have a diminishing effect. I am more interested in—well, it's always back to Whitman, right?—incorporating worlds, utilizing different tonalities and textures, and having moments that jolt or stun a reader. These moments do not happen in easy succession or all at once; instead, they are moments or flashes a reader might not quite understand—"Oh! What is that?"—but a reader is going to feel like "I want to understand this more, I'm going to come back." Unlike a short poem, a sequence keeps unfolding, and, yes, there will be slacker moments, more narrative moments, lyrical moments, dramatic moments; they will be woven together, and *then* the reader is going to say, "Hmm, I need to reread this again, I want to understand this more." And hopefully each time, more emerges.

TL: When I'm reading your longer poems, I do have those moments when I am startled or surprised. And the reaction is visceral. But I never know where this is going to happen. These shocks, for example, do not always happen at the end of a poem.

AS: Absolutely. If I said I wanted the end of each section to stun or startle a reader, that intention becomes programmatic. And, in writing, one would then confine the possibilities of the poem, because one would have the need to go in a certain direction, whereas for me one great thing about poetry is I'm always discovering, I'm shedding where I think the poem is going. I might start with an impulse and then find, "this isn't it at all, the real poem is somewhere else." And so I'm constantly discovering. I want those shocks to be there, but I myself writing them don't quite know where they are: they get discovered along the way.

TL: I'm looking at a book like *Quipu*, which is really a mix of shorter, one-page poems and longer poems. Do you know in advance which poems will be shorter, concise movements and which ones will be serial pieces? Or does the serial poem come about because along the way you think, "I haven't said every-thing I wanted to say yet"?

AS: I don't plan out in advance. I sometimes write a short poem and think, wait a minute, the end is just the beginning. I liken it to a stone from an archi-pelago that is beginning to emerge above surface, and I often intuit there's much more below that I need to mine and explore and develop. Although I don't sit down and say, "Now I'm going to write a sequence," sometimes I feel enormous inner pressure and guess that I will write something long. At other times, I will write several poems and find they're interconnected, and then those poems become the core to something larger. When I wrote "Apache Plume," I really just had this outpouring of emotion, and then, after writing many separate poems, I laid them out on the floor and thought, "they're all interconnected in ways I could not have envisioned beforehand, they should be moved together." And when I wrote the tenth and last poem, the other nine poems were already there.

TL: You have a tendency in some of your other serial poems to include sections that might not hold up at all on their own. Such as some of the listing poems.

AS: That's right.

TL: Are such poems like interludes that corral some of the themes and imagery in the longer poems?

AS: I think different principles and rationales are at work and it's hard for me to articulate it from the inside out, but I'm interested in—and I'm thinking of the list of endangered species in "The String Diamond"—suspending narration. I love the sounds to those plants. I had a list of 500 endangered species from *National Geographic* and played with the names, and it became an articulation of pure sound. From one point of view, it was an elegy, mourning species that are vanishing off the face of the earth, but, from another point of view, each one of these species is unique, is still here and still exerting its presence. And where that moment of revelation can happen in a poem is endlessly fascinating to me. If "The String Diamond" sequence started with the list, it would have no narration to suspend, but having set in motion a game of go, it's as if the naming—creating a litany or spell or incantation with language—is also trying to suspend time.

TL: Oddly—and I'm not trying to be contrary here—I find that list poem reads like an independent poem. You could have titled it and it would have been able to stand on its own. A reader can deconstruct those names, too, to see if they are leading somewhere.

AS: That's interesting. I certainly had not envisioned that. One thing that interests me is how you can have an enormous disparity between the intention and the effect. And that's actually a good thing. When I was writing the list of names in "The String Diamond," I was thinking, "This is like placing stones along a line on a go board; it's like linear thinking and you're doomed." But you're saying it's a complete poem in itself, and hearing you say that, I agree, though I had not thought of this before.

TL: This poem was not what I was thinking of when I mentioned that in your serial poems you tend to include pieces that really only make sense when contextualized with the larger sequence. I was thinking of section five of "Kaiseki," where you begin, "They searched and searched for a loggerhead shrike." I don't think this would stand alone as easily as the list poem of the names of endangered plants.

AS: Yes, sure. The fragments in section five of "Kaiseki" can't stand alone; they require the larger context of the sequence. And yet it's fascinating how some sections of a sequence can have a large degree of autonomy, while others can't. I think it has to do with the relationship between part and whole, but it's still mysterious.

TL: Yet you appear to have quite a handle on the things you're trying to achieve with your poems. I get the sense, for example, that when you are citing certain scientific and cultural references in your poems that you are aware most readers will find them strange. The fact that you supply notes indicates that you're aware of this.

AS: Right. There are bare, skeletal notes, but at least they are like pointers or directions to pursue. I don't want the allusions or references to other disciplines and other endeavors to become too much of an obstacle. I'm trying to negotiate that sense of inviting the reader to stretch a little bit, hoping they will make that effort, because I believe it's rewarding in the end. You asked that wonderful question about balancing accessibility and difficulty and I do try and approach the poem with the understanding that I don't want the reader to necessarily have knowledge of contemporary physics or mycology—in some ways that knowledge might actually be a hindrance. Without knowing anything, you can be more open and discover and experience more.

TL: So, in introducing the reader to the unfamiliar you're trying to get that reader to pay attention to the act of reading and the apprehension of reading.

AS: Absolutely.

TL: One of my favorite poems of yours is the aforementioned "Apache Plume." In the third section, "The Names of a Bird," you write, "If you know / the names of a bird in ten languages, do you know // any more about the bird?" That gave me pause. I felt it to be true and not a little sad. Could you discuss this passage, not only in terms of its place in the poem but in relation to the rest of your work?"

AS: I consider "Apache Plume" a suite rather than a sequence. Each section, with a subtitle, is autonomous, unlike a numbered section in a sequence. In "Apache Plume," I wrote ten love poems to my wife, Carol Moldaw, and the third poem, "The Names of a Bird," explores the relationship between "I" and "you." In the passage you've quoted, the speaker is exploring the possibilities of knowledge, connection, and intimacy. If someone names a bird in ten languages, that naming is a lateral motion: it doesn't bring the namer any closer to what is named, and so connection and intimacy are not possible. If the poem ended there, it would indeed be sad, but the speaker instinctively recognizes this impasse and proceeds to personalize experience through memory: "I recollect how you folded a desert willow blossom // into a notebook ... I know what it is to touch the mole between your breasts." Here the speaker arrives at a place where contact and intimacy are possible. He does not yet verbalize it—it will happen at the end of section seven with, "I know this instant moment which is ours"—because his intelligence doesn't fully comprehend it. This moment that communicates before it's understood is about poetry as well as love.

The passage about naming birds in ten languages is important in relation to the rest of my work, because it raises the large issues of naming, knowledge, and connection. I've already asserted that in "The Names of a Bird," a lateral motion of naming would not help the speaker gain any knowledge about the bird itself, but what if naming enacted a vertical rather than a horizontal motion? In section three of "The String Diamond," I created a vocalization of imminent loss. And in section five of "Spectral Line," I list forty American Indian tribes. Here the list embodies the names of students I had the privilege to teach at the Institute, and the procession of names is a roll call. If "The String Diamond" and "Spectral Line" contained only the sections of names, they would go nowhere, but context is crucial. In "The String Diamond," nonlinear connections form webs and allow meaning to accrue, while linear connection arrives at a dead end. So I believe the passage of lateral naming in "The Names of a Bird" reveals the limitations of impersonal knowledge. As a poet, I find that I zigzag between objective observation and subjective experience and need to "personalize the way" so that the poem can become a living force.

TL: In the fourth section of your poem "Before Completion," you begin with a startling juxtaposition: "a poet describes herding pigs/beside a girl with a glass eye and affirms/the power to dream and transform. Later,/in exile, he axes his wife and hangs himself." Your poems are filled with such juxtapositions that, at first, shock and then, upon further inspection, seem less shocking than true—and possible. Could you talk about your use of juxtapositions?

AS: Juxtaposition is an essential tool at my disposal. It can surprise, intensify, suspend, disrupt, or reinforce, and I'd like to make a distinction between juxtaposition in stillness (space) and juxtaposition in motion (time). Juxtaposition in stillness occurs where two fragments or segments are placed side by side. Here I liken the effect to magnetism: the two pieces can attract, repel, or undergo varying degrees of attraction or repulsion. A series of fragments can create a disorienting, even bewildering, field of energy, but this experience may be a necessary stage. Juxtaposition in motion occurs when a narrative is telescoped or when two or more narratives are spun together and converge. I liken juxtaposition in motion to moments in a Shakespearean play where a subplot throws light on and exerts psychological force on the main plot. Juxtaposition in stillness is like the moment on stage when charged silence fills the air. In either case, juxtaposition has a dramatic value; it involves tension and co-existent fields of energy.

In other interviews, I've mentioned that Chinese characters are created through juxtaposition, and that these juxtapositions create rich and mysterious effects. If you write the character "sun," and then, to the right, the character "moon," you create the character "bright." If you write the character "field," and below, the character "heart/mind," you create the character "think." Notice how physical thought becomes in this language system: to think is to put your heart and mind into a field. In contrast to the juxtapositions inside of Chinese characters that frequently connect and clarify, my juxtapositions are frequently jarring and dissonant; yet, I am, in my own way, also searching for deep connection.

In the passage you quoted from "Before Completion," the lines are shockingly true. In 1985, I met the Misty poet, Gu Cheng, in Beijing, and we became friends. During the Cultural Revolution, he and his father herded pigs in the countryside. Years later, after Tiananmen, in exile in New Zealand, he axed his wife and hanged himself. In the poem, I telescoped many years and juxtaposed the early incident with the later one to compress and intensify the tragic story.

TL: In that same section you write: "Do the transformations of memory / become the changing lines of divination?" Elsewhere, such as in "Aqueous Gold" from Quipu, you refer to how the memory can "batter and renew," how it is impoverished, and, perhaps most stunningly, how "thoughts inch through" it "the way maggots do a cèpe." Do you have a theory of memory? How does memory function in one to transform and, possibly, transcend?

AS: I don't have a theory of memory, but I'm interested in how memory is a living force within us all. Memory is a way of unfolding and processing human experience, and it's also invention. Who we are in the present is significantly related to our past, and the wider the range, and the greater the emotional depth and imaginative power to recreate those experiences, the richer, more various and creative we are and can be. As we tap into deep memories, we live more fully in the present. In addition, if one has lived through tragedy, struggling with memories often becomes a process by which one works toward reconciliation and peace. If one dwells too much on these memories, one can become trapped, and then "thoughts inch through / memory the way maggots inch through a cèpe"; but when memories have singularity, they can also be Wordworth's "spots of time" that nourish and sustain.

TL: "Aqueous Gold" is one of my favorite poems of yours. I particularly admire the ways you explore memory there.

AS: To me, "Aqueous Gold" is an exploration of desire and memory. Those are two axes in my poetry. One thinks one's going forward in desire but that can be illusory; one thinks one's going backwards in memory, but memory is also invention.

TL: In its references to air and water, I see portions of "Aqueous Gold" as linked to Pre-Socratic thought.

AS: Pre-Socratic thinking is a huge influence upon me. I see all of those philosophers as poets: Thales, Parmenides, etc... From a scientific point of view we can say their views of the world—that the world is air or the world is fire—are ridiculous. And yet you read a fragment of Heraclitus and it's like wow, where did that come from, it's so poetic, it's so original.

TL: Perhaps part of the appeal to this group of philosophers may be that all we have are the fragments, that a complete system of thought is lacking, which enables us to project on to their aphorisms and propositions our own intellectual and creative visions.

AS: I think those fragments are tantalizing and provocative, and a great place for any poet to go to. Plato for me is so fully fleshed out it becomes problematical, there isn't room—whereas, as you say, with the fragments and the gaps, that space is supremely useful. When Thales says "Earth rests upon water" a scientist might balk, but a poet might think what he's really saying, through metaphor, is that there is no absolute foundation; and this is true and something I can make use of.

TL: Space seems to be an important factor in your compositional methods, too. No matter how much you extend a poem into several sections, I never sense your poems are overwritten. In fact, I often leave your poems with more questions than answers, that there is a lot of space left.

AS: Thank you. I take this as a huge compliment that you sense that spaciousness.

TL: Is it a challenge for you to create this kind of space?

AS: It is, and frankly there are often sections to the sequences that don't make it in to the final poem because I want the reader to experience that kind of space that keeps opening up. Sometimes there are passages where I realize I was just thinking out some things that are enacted more effectively in other sections, so those passages are removed. I love taking sections and laying them out on the floor, putting blank sheets of paper between them, and asking, What happens if I spread these apart? Could something go here that is unanticipated? Or what happens if I bring them together? So I am constantly testing the spacial relations inside of the poem, which is connected to time, of course, as the poem unfolds, as one reads it.

TL: So even when you've written a poetic sequence that is cohesive or has clear linkages, you often deliberately try to break them, that you're more interested in creating further spaces between the links.

AS: That's right.

TL: And yet, ironically, the more you expand your poems the more space appears to be in them.

AS: That is, again, a huge compliment. It's like worlds inside of a world. I want the rigor of the poem to be there. I don't want it to feel like "Oh, this is a book-length project." This is one of the reasons I've resisted writing a book-length poem or sequence, although the temptation is there, and so many poets are doing it. Instead of consciously embarking on a book project, I'd rather write thirty sections and realize later that only ten can truly work together.

TL: Your use of the couplet seems quite useful in creating that sense of space.

AS: I started to use the couplet when I found my poems were leaping a lot. If the poem was laid out in a block-like, one-stanza form, the leaps were jammed together. When I opened the poem into couplets, the white space allowed more breathing room so that a reader could, at the end of the couplet, not only have the slight pause at the end of a line but also a breathing space before the next leap. I want to add that I have found the couplet form supremely helpful for editing: in a block-like form, I sometimes have difficulty seeing clunky or over-written phrases; whereas, in couplet form, it is much easier to spot phrases that need to be cut or reworked. So I find myself writing drafts of poems in couplet form. Sometimes I will compress all the two-line stanzas into one stanza, some-times the poem requires a different shape, but, frequently, because the couplets are integrated into the process of creation, the final poem stays in that form.

TL: How does gingko light serve as a structural and thematic metaphor for the book *The Gingko Light?*

AS: The image of the ginkgo appears and disappears throughout the book. It first appears as a fossil image, then some of its history—"once thought extinct, the ginkgo / was discovered in Himalayan monasteries // and propagated back into the world"—is revealed. The history culminates in the passage where, after the atom bomb is dropped on Hiroshima, a ginkgo tree survives and flowers. In our challenged and challenging world, faced with the extinction of so many living species, the ginkgo's response becomes a metaphor for how we might live. In addition, the endlessly branching venation pattern of the ginkgo leaf informs the book: the first vein at the base of the leaf, or, equivalently, at the spine of the book, is the catalog of Native tribes in "Spectral Line." The catalog is not only located at the center of that sequence, but it is also located at the center of the book. But my book is not called *The Ginkgo Tree*. I was after a mythic title, and the phrase—the ginkgo light—embodied, for me, the precarious splendor of our world.

TL: As we wrap up, I am wondering if you wish to address anything else.

AS: Well, with reference to one of your earlier questions, I was really glad you asked me how I situated myself in the tradition of American poetry, because so often categories such as Asian American poetry or Native American poetry get used in ways that aren't helpful. I wondered about raising the issue that all these categories should be seen as aspects of one poetry—American poetry. Maybe one of the difficulties right now is that things are artificially divided up. I don't see why an anthology of American literature, for instance, can't start with the Navajo Nightway Chant.

TL: Clearly you are so much more than an American poet who is cognizant of the poetic traditions of China. In this chat alone you've mentioned Whitman more than once. How do you see yourself as participating in this larger story of American poetry?

AS: I have a significant connection to Whitman, Emerson, Williams, Pound, and Stevens. I believe that—and I'm borrowing another metaphor here— growth is at the edge of a leaf, and that as today's growth is incorporated into tomorrow's tradition, we, as contemporary poets, are central to it, adding to the tradition and great richness of American poetry.

III · LANDSCAPE AS AUTOBIOGRAPHY

ACEQUIAS AS QUIPUS, QUIPUS AS POEMS,
by Arthur Sze (2019)

FOR THE LAST FORTY-FIVE YEARS, I have lived in Northern New Mexico; during this time, I've been involved with two acequias: the Ancon de Jacona and the Acequia del Llano. The word "acequia" is derived from the Arabic *as-saquiya* and refers to the irrigation ditch, as well as the association of members connected to it, that transports water from a river to farms and fields. For eighteen years, I was involved with the Ancon de Jacona, twenty miles north of Santa Fe, and, for the last four years, I have been actively involved with the Acequia del Llano.

The Acequia del Llano is the youngest of the four acequias that run through the city of Santa Fe. It is 1.5 miles long and begins at Nichols Reservoir and runs eventually into the Santa Fe River. Fourteen members are in this ditch association, and the acequia irrigates about thirty acres of gardens and orchards. In this environment, some of the endangered and threatened species that draw on this watershed include the southwestern willow fly catcher, the least tern, the violet-crowned hummingbird, the American marten, and the white-tailed ptarmigan. Other wildlife in the area include deer, black bear, coyotes, turkeys, and quail.

As a *parciante*, or voting member of the acequia, I am actively involved in the maintenance of this ditch. Just last week, on April 7, all of the members came, or hired workers who came, to do the annual spring ditch cleaning; this involves walking the length of the ditch, from reservoir to river, cleaning, with shovels and clippers, branches, silt, and other debris that has accumulated over the late fall and winter.

The ditch association is organized with a *mayordomo*, ditch manager, who oversees the distribution of water according to each *parciante's* amount of water rights and also verifies that each *parciante* follows the strict days and times of the watering schedule. The current *mayordomo*, Mike Cruz, drives periodically up and down Canyon Road and monitors the usage to make sure no water is being wasted and spilling into the street. The rules of the acequia are that if someone upstream is not using water during their allotted time, someone downstream can draw on that water. However, one cannot draw on water when someone downstream has the right to that water. The *mayordomo* resolves any conflicts about water usage, and he also has the authority to fine land owners who do not abide by the rules. For our land, we have two days a week when we can draw water: from Thursday at 6 p.m. to Friday morning at 7:30 a.m., and from Sunday at 6 a.m. to Monday at 6 a.m.

The acequia runs at a higher elevation than all of the land held by the *parciantes*, so the flow of water is gravity fed. On Thursdays and Sundays, I walk about a quarter of a mile uphill to the ditch and drop a metal gate into it. Water then backs up, and as the level rises, water goes down two pipes. Two large green holding tanks fill, and then water runs into a complex system of pipes set with timers, so sprinklers water grass, a garden, a few hundred-year-old apple trees, and flower beds around the house, according to the different zones and times. I manually turn on and move a secondary set of rotating sprinklers to water the orchard that has apple, peach, and pear trees.

New Mexico is a very dry landscape, and, this year, due to climate change, the drought is particularly damaging. By July 1, the annual rainfall is normally 4.5 inches, and, as I write today on July 5, the annual rainfall is an astoundingly low 1.25 inches. Severe water-conservation measures are in effect throughout the city, and everyone who has the right to draw water off the Acequia del Llano is aware how precious this resource is, and the sharing of this irrigation water actively promotes community needs over a single individual need. It also serves as an important reminder and contrast to our consumer culture where, as Ezra Pound once observed, "[Nothing] is made to endure nor to live with / but [...] to sell and sell quickly." During the Depression, there are stories of impoverished families sharing sheep bones to flavor broth. Just like the water that was passed along the irrigation line, bones were passed from family to family to flavor subsistence soup.

Each year the irrigation season runs from about April 15 to October 15. In April, as I get up in the dark in the early morning and walk uphill to divert water from the ditch, I notice Venus, Orion, and other constellations of stars. I see lights from a dozen houses, on the far side of the Santa Fe River, flickering in the darkness. As it moves toward summer, I notice the constellations shift in the sky, and, by July 1, when I walk uphill, I am walking in early daylight. By mid-September, I will again be using a flashlight to head uphill in the dark and will be listening for deer or coyote in between the piñons and junipers. Connected to this seasonal rhythm, I am in biweekly contact with flowing water and recognize, as a steward, it is a privilege to use it to irrigate the land. This liminal awareness sparked my poem, "First Snow":

FIRST SNOW

A rabbit has stopped on the gravel driveway:

 imbibing the silence,
 you stare at spruce needles:

   there's no sound of a leaf blower,
   no sign of a black bear;

a few weeks ago, a buck scraped his rack
 against an aspen trunk;
 a carpenter scribed a plank along a curved stone wall.

  You only spot the rabbit's ears and tail:

when it moves, you locate it against speckled gravel,
but when it stops, it blends in again;

 the world of being is like this gravel:

   you think you own a car, a house,
   this blue-zigzagged shirt, but you just borrow these things.

Yesterday, you constructed an aqueduct of dreams
  and stood at Gibraltar,
     but you possess nothing.

Snow melts into a pool of clear water;
 and, in this stillness,

   starlight behind daylight wherever you gaze.

If you take an aerial view and visualize the acequia running along the hillside as a primary flow and then locate the many subsidiary or secondary, flows running downhill, perpendicularly, from the main flow, to irrigate various orchards and fields, you will see a quipu composed of water. In Inca culture, a quipu is made out of spun fiber and is defined in the *Merriam Webster's Collegiate Dictionary* as: "a device made of a main cord with smaller varicolored cords attached and knotted and used by the ancient Peruvians (as for calculating)."

 The word quipu has two spellings: the older version, quipu, is based on the Spanish spelling for the Quechua word that means "knot." It is more often spelled "khipu" today. In either case, the quipu is usually made of cotton; it is lightweight, portable, and encodes information. There are two kinds of quipus:

numerical and non-numerical. The numerical ones record accounting information. Researchers have examined the knotting in quipus, and they are able to read the numbers, one to nine. The location of knots on the numerically-based cords follows a base-ten decimal system, so a quipu can easily incorporate ones, tens, hundreds, and thousands. For instance, a quipu that accounted for containers of potatoes in a mountainside storage vault would be invaluable during a famine. The rulers could pull potatoes out from storage, feed people, and retie the knots, so that inventories of food could be kept up to date. Numerical quipus track numbers of sandals, gold, census numbers of people living in a village, and so on, so these quipus provide essential day-to-day information that helped the Inca rulers respond to crises and rule the kingdom.

Interestingly, poet and translator Brenda Hillman has mentioned that water usage in the Sahara was tracked by tying and untying knots. And there is also evidence of ancient Chinese quipus, composed of silk, that predate Chinese characters. In the next-to-last chapter of the *Dao De Jing*, there is a passage that says, let people go back to communicating through knotted cords. In a poem, "Thoughts," by Du Fu, in the Tang dynasty, the speaker sits on a porch at night and muses how people struggle futilely for glory, and then the speaker considers how someone started communicating by knotting cords and now there's the mire and endless bureaucracy of government! So the use of knotted cords as a vehicle for communication can be found in many ancient cultures.

Focusing on the non-numerical quipus, the possibility they encode language is tantalizing, but, so far, no one has been able to "read" or decipher them; the knotting does not follow a linear base-ten accounting system. Nevertheless, several important historical accounts provide evidence that quipus incorporate narrative information that encodes the myths, legends and histories of the Incas. One important historical account describes an Inca runner who arrives at a remote mountain village. He pulls out a quipu, and a *quipucamayoc*, a specialized reader of quipus, looks at it. The village then begins a revolt against the Spanish. Here, then, is evidence that the quipu must have contained narrative information.

As a poet, the non-numerical quipus interest me most. I like to think of the knotting in a quipu as a physical and visual reminder of the way a word or phrase may be repeated and turned in a poem. Robert Fitzgerald once remarked that repetition in Homer utilized elegant variation, that each time the repeat occurred, the word was enriched and deepened in meaning.

In composing my book, *Quipu*, I looked at all the dictionary definitions of the word "as" and noted ten different meanings. In the title poem "Quipu," a sequence of nine poems, I took it upon myself to keep using the word "as" and, over time, allowing different meanings to accrue. This was an organic way to layer, deepen, and simultaneously enrich the meaning of the poem. The poet Cole Swenson has noted that repetition frequently involved casting a spell. I agree and would add that repetition can also become a form of insistence. The knots can refer to repeats of words, and they can also refer to repeats in syntactic patterns; moreover, as in a quipu where the spin of fiber in secondary cords can shift from clockwise to counter-clockwise, I envisioned a shift where nouns could turn into verbs. The sequence "Quipu" is too long to reprint here, but some of these thematic currents are clearly initiated in the opening section:

QUIPU

1.

I try to see a bald eagle nest in a Douglas fir
but catch my sleeve on thorns, notice blackberries,

hear large wings splashing water in a lagoon.
I glimpse a heron perched on a post above a tidal flat,

remember red elderberries arcing along a path
where you catch and release a newt among ferns.

And as a doe slips across the road behind us,
we zigzag when we encounter a point of resistance,

zigzag as if we describe the edge of an immense leaf,
as if we plumb a jagged coastline where tides

wash and renew the mind. I stare at abalone eyes,
am startled at how soft a sunflower star is to touch,

how sticky a tentacle of an anemone is to finger.
When we walk barefoot in sand, I sway

to the motion of waves, mark bits of crabs
washed to shore, see—in an instant a dog wrenches

a leash around the hand of a woman, shatters bones—
ensuing loss salamanders the body, lagoons the mind.

✠

The flow of water is also the flow of language: water and poetry are essential movements that affirm and shape life. Water can be conceived of as beginningless beginning and endless end; if water has no shape of its own, it can take any shape and has infinite possibility. In poetry, I am interested in a finite thing that has a multiple or polysemous range of expression and meaning. Poetry utilizes a finite set of words and yet has the possibility of reaching into the infinite, and it calls our attention to the mystery of existence. I am reminded of Dogen's dictum, "Water is the koan of water." If water is a riddle of itself, then all of creation is mysterious and marvelous. It is astonishing life exists and that there is anything at all.

In looking back over my time in New Mexico, I realize that the scarcity of water has helped me pay close attention to living details and the profoundly changing landscape. This realization is embodied in a poem of mine set in Jacona:

RED BREATH

Shaggy red clouds in the west—

unlatching a gate, I step into a field:
   no coyote slants across with a chicken in its mouth,

   no wild asparagus rises near the ditch.

In the night sky, Babylonian astronomers
   recorded a supernova
   and witnessed the past catch up to the present,

   but they did not write
      what they felt at what they saw—

they could not see to this moment.
From August, we could not see to this moment

   but draw water out of a deep well—
   it has the taste of

   creek water in a tin cup,
      and my teeth ache against the cold.

Juniper smoke rises and twists through the flue—

   my eyes widen
   as I brush your hair, brush your hair—

   I have red breath:
   in the deep night, we are again lit,
      and I true this time to consequence.

Another time, walking in the ditch of the Ancon de Jacona before spring cleaning, I marveled at the landscape around me and, in imagination, moved across space and time. The village of Jacona is in an agricultural valley fed by the Pojoaque River, and Los Alamos, the birthplace of our atomic age, sits visibly on a mesa to the west. The following poem is in an invented form. Starting with the title, each line picks up a word or words from the previous line, and, at the end, a word is picked up, again, in the title, so my form embodies line and circle. In a similar way, an irrigation ditch in northern New Mexico that carries water to the fields forms line and circle; it marks the seasonal beginning and end that supports and sustains life here.

SIGHT LINES

I'm walking in sight of the Río Nambe—

salt cedar rises through silt in an irrigation ditch—

the snowpack in the Sangre de Cristos has already dwindled before spring—

at least no fires erupt in the conifers above Los Alamos—

the plutonium waste has been hauled to an underground site—

a man who built plutonium triggers breeds horses now—

no one could anticipate this distance from Monticello—

Jefferson despised newspapers, but no one thing takes us out of ourselves—

during the Cultural Revolution, a boy saw his mother shot in front of a
    firing squad—

a woman detonates when a spam text triggers bombs strapped to her body—

when I come to an upright circular steel lid, I step out of the ditch—

I step out of the ditch but step deeper into myself—

I arrive at a space that no longer needs autumn or spring—

I find ginseng where there is no ginseng my talisman of desire—

though you are visiting Paris, you are here at my fingertips—

though I step back into the ditch, no whitening cloud dispels this world's
    mystery—

the ditch ran before the year of the Louisiana Purchase—

I'm walking on silt, glimpsing horses in the field—

fielding the shapes of our bodies in white sand—

though parallel lines touch in the infinite, the infinite is here—

IV · CULTURAL PERSPECTIVES

THE STREAMS STREAMING THROUGH US:
The Rich Diversity of Asian American Poetry, A Talk at the Library of Congress by Arthur Sze (2020)

IT IS A PLEASURE AND HONOR to give what can be best described as an intimate walk through Asian American literary history from my personal experience and perspective.

In 2014, Lawrence-Minh Davis and Gerald Maa, the editors of *AALR*, [*Asian American Literary Review*], invited me to engage in "A Lettre Fellowship Program to nurture emerging Asian American writers and grow community across literary generations." I accepted their invitation and corresponded with Ocean Vuong, two years before he was to publish his celebrated book, *Night Sky With Exit Wounds*. We exchanged three sets of letters, and, at the outset, Ocean immediately articulated his Asian American identity through language. He wrote:"I am starting to think that to be an Asian American is to build one's own nation—within one's body. And maybe my best tools happen to be words and language. Through language, my nation remains malleable, ever changing, and borderless. My citizens are words and words belong to all who use them." I've made only one out of an enormous number of possible selections to highlight the rich diversity of Asian American poetry, through the stream of personal experience.

I'm going to begin with a brief biographical sketch. As the son of Chinese immigrants from Beijing, I grew up in suburbia, in Garden City, New York. I felt a lot of pressure to pursue something in the sciences or engineering, and I came to poetry rather late. As a freshman at MIT, bored in a calculus lecture, I wrote my first poem. Soon I was writing all the time. In my sophomore year, Denise Levertov came from California and taught a poetry workshop. She made the Bay Area sound exciting, and I transferred to the University of California at Berkeley. There, Josephine Miles became my mentor. Derek Walcott once said to me that because the path of a poet is arduous, there is always someone who tells a young poet that poetry is worth committing to. For him, it was his mother; for me, it was Josephine Miles.

After I graduated from UC Berkeley, I moved to Santa Fe, New Mexico, and joined the New Mexico Poetry-in-the-Schools program. The group of poets I met in that program included Mei-mei Berssenbrugge. Mei-mei and I have been friends since 1973, and, over the years, we have shared drafts of poems at countless lunches, talked about poetry while we hiked from the bottom of the

Santa Fe ski basin to the top of Lake Peak (12,409 feet above sea level), and, for a few years, as faculty at the Institute of American Indian Arts when the budget was tight, we even shared an office. During that time, we were also contributing editors to a small, experimental literary magazine, *Tyuonyi* (a Keresan word that means "the meeting place") that sought to bring multicultural poetic perspectives into conversation with each other.

I've picked the opening of a relatively early poem of Mei-mei's, "Chinese Space," with its signature long line, like the horizon line stretching across a mesa in Northern New Mexico, even though the place described here is in China:

> First there is the gate from the street, then some flowers inside the wall,
> then the inner, roofed gate. It is a very plain wall, without expressionistic
>   means,
> such as contrasting light on paving stones inside the courtyard to the
>   calligraphed foundation stones.
> My grandfather called this the façade or Baroque experience, rendering a
>   courtyard transparent.
> The eye expecting to confront static space experiences a lavish range of
>   optical events,
> such as crickets in Ming jars, their syncopation like the right, then left, then
>   right progress
> into the house, an experience that cannot be sustained in consciousness,
>   because
> your movement itself binds passing time, more than entering directs it.

From Mei-mei, I heard about Basement Workshop in New York City and met Jessica Hagedorn, who was curating the poetry series there. Here's the opening to "Picture This," (after a series of paintings titled *Gift Wrapped Dolls*, by James Rosenquist):

> A woman hurled. Hurled out.
> A woman
> hurls herself out the window
> exits out
> the window
> expects to   crashland
> on the sidewalk
> crashland
> bones and skin
> into sidewalk
> below

Through Basement Workshop, I also met Frances Chung and Kimiko Hahn. Admiring Kimiko's adaptations of the Japanese form *zuihitsu*, or "running brush," I've chosen this passage from "Opening Her Text":

I nestle with my daughter in her bed in the room painted pink a decade ago; half the pink, now covered with glossy clippings of this or that star, male and female. Her reading light spots a book in my hands.

She is the oldest of two daughters and on the verge of one of those beginnings. Remove. Approach. (Reproach?)

Outside boys kill one another over sharp lyrics. Girls slash strangers across the face. In Prospect Park the fireflies begin their mating flares while other insects settle into moist foliage.

As I became better known as a poet, I started to travel, and, in 1985, met Pat Matsueda in Honolulu. Pat has served for years as managing editor of *Manoa: A Pacific Journal of International Writing*. The undertow of her poem, "Shika (Deer) Shrine, Japan," *for my sister,* has stayed with me:

Two years old,
you have a mouth like a split plum.
Our mother is braced against a tree,
trying to conceal her wound.
Oblivious, we follow our father
beneath the ironwoods,
through the stains of shadows on the ground.
In silence,
we feed the deer
at Shika Shrine.

On that trip, I had lunch with Wing Tek Lum in Honolulu, Chinatown, and we discovered we shared an admiration for the ancient Chinese poet, Tao Qian; in fact, a line from one of Tao's poems was displayed prominently in his office. Here's an excerpt from "To a Poet Who Says He's Stopped Writing (Temporarily)":

These periods are as essential
as that moment you sit down in a rush
your favorite pen in hand
pulling out that journal
     you've always carried for this very purpose

And when the point scratches surface
flesh is made word
and these small truths of your existence
illumine the page
    like laser light, scorching our hearts forever

During this time, I joined the board of a small press, Tooth of Time Books, located in Guadalupita, New Mexico. The founder, John Brandi, had reissued my first book and also published my second book of poetry. I looked for books by emerging poets and sponsored Carolyn Lau's *Wode Shuofa: My Way of Speaking* that was published in 1988. Here's Carolyn's quirky, calligraphic style in a complete short poem, "Being Chinese in English":

The man in the night reading by lamplight.
Nearby, the men playing checkers.

All the varieties of crickets: nervous, cringing.

The balcony gardens insisting
we better not show
our interest in orgasm.

Outside, babies questioning their ears; therefore,
shifting twilight upside down
in softspots.

Dear Ox, how desperate we are,
certain only in this thing we can call ours
urging life to feel so good in pleasure.

At Tooth of Time, I also helped to publish another first book by an Asian American poet, *cir'cum·nav'i·ga'tion*, by Cyn Zarco. Here's the opening stanza to her book:

Gustavo said,
"Your poems are like samba,
some even tango on the page
as if part of some strange ritual—
what the rooster does before mounting.

Living in New Mexico, I found connection to other Asian American poets through publication. When Joseph Bruchac edited and published his groundbreaking anthology *Breaking Silence* in 1983, I found myself in the company of so many poets I admired. And a decade later, Garrett Hongo's anthology, *The Open Boat*, brought many of us a wider audience.

Here's the opening to Garrett's "Obon: *Dance for the Dead*" that begins with the important work of reclamation:

> I have no memories or photograph of my father
> coming home from war, thin as a caneworker,
> a splinter of flesh in his olive greens
> and khakis and spit-shined G.I. shoes;
>
> Or of my grandfather in his flower-print shirt,
> humming his bar-tunes, tying the bandana
> to his head to hold the sweat back from his face
> as he bent to weed and hoe the garden that Sunday
> while swarms of planes maneuvered overhead.

Around this time, I also developed a friendship with Marilyn Chin. I first came across her translations of the Chinese modernist poet, Ai Qing. Many of her poems are informed by a knowledge of classical Chinese poetry, and here she adapts the *fu*, or rhyme prose form, in this passage from "Rhapsody in Plain Yellow":

> Say: A scentless camellia bush bloodied the afternoon.
>   Fuck this line, can you really believe this?
> When did I become the master of suburban bliss?
>   With whose tongue were we born?
> The language of the masters is the language of the aggressors.
>   We've studied their cadence carefully—
>
> enrolled in a class to *improve our accent,*
>   Meanwhile, they hover over, waiting for us to stumble ...
> to drop an article, mispronounce an R.
>   Say: softly, softly, the silent gunboats glide.

During the mid-1980s, I met Cathy Song several times when she came to Santa Fe. Her husband's family lived in town, and we used to meet at a local coffee shop. She was completing her second collection, *Frameless Windows, Squares of Light*. I remember she talked about how it was a struggle to be a mother and balance those demands with invitations for readings and workshops. And she prioritized her family. Here's the opening to "Litany":

She gave you the names of things,
each word, a candle
you held between yourself and the dark.
The litany of the alphabet
like a rosary before sleep.
Then the shadows on the wall
became familiar,
the storybook shape of elephants.

In 1981, the University of California at Berkeley held an Asian American
literary festival, and I met John Yau there. We developed an abiding friendship
and shared an enthusiasm for the difficult and challenging Tang dynasty poets,
Li Shangyin and Li He, as well as Surrealism and experimental poetry. He came
out to Santa Fe several times, and we usually stopped in at a few art galleries.
On one visit I told John I had met Agnes Martin, and he wondered if we could
drive out to Galisteo to see where she lived. I didn't know Agnes well enough to
call her, but I knew where her house was. I drove John out and remember he was
so excited to take a few photographs from the road of her adobe house and the
surrounding landscape.

John often writes in sequences, and I've selected the last section to
"Borrowed Love Poems":

Now that the seven wonders of the night
have been stolen by history

Now that the sky is lost and the stars
have slipped into a book

Now that the moon is boiling
like the blood where it swims

Now that there are no blossoms left
to glue to the sky

What can I do,
I who never invented anything

and who dreamed of you so much
I was amazed to discover

the claw marks of those
who preceded us across this burning floor

In the 1990s, I met Walter Lew in New York. Walter was the editor-in-chief at Kaya Production and assembled a sprawling anthology of Asian American Poetry, *Premonitions*. He wanted to widen the range of aesthetics to include "the astonishing diversity and eloquence of new poetries spread out among numerous networks and poetics, both esoteric and activist, imagist and deconstructive, pidgin and purist, diasporic and Americanist, high literary and pop cultural."

Here's the ending from Walter's opening poem in *Treadwinds,* which is, as every poem is, an ars poetica and includes the French word, *faits,* or facts, and even borrows a phrase, "lake of the heart," from Dante:

> We make our laws up out of
>
> > fear and tenacity
> > and find in them
> > *faits* about the light, its
> > aberration and flawing
> > Whenever a planet
>
> Wheels all hell-like
> Grinding in the wrong
>
> > [Azimuth or angle of
> > Right-ascension: coordinates
>
> Deep in the lake of the heart.

On a trip to Minneapolis, I reached out to David Mura, and we had lunch together. I believe it was shortly after he published his second book, *The Colors of Desire*. Here is the opening from the title poem, "1 *Photograph of a Lynching* (circa 1930)"

> These men? In their dented felt hats,
> in the way their fingers tug their suspenders or vests,
> with faces a bit puffy or too lean, eyes narrow and close together,
> they seem too like our image of the South,
> the Thirties. Of course they are white;
> who then could create this cardboard figure, face
> flat and grey, eyes oversized, bulging like
> an ancient totem this gang has dug up?

Around this time I came into contact with Eileen Tabios, who was active with the Asian American Writers Workshop. Eileen interviewed me about my poem "Archipelago," and our discussion gave her the idea to interview fifteen Asian American poets. She assembled the anthology *Black Lightning: Poetry-in-Progress*, and the Writers Workshop published it in 1998. This was the first anthology to share working drafts of poems as well as interviews with each poet.

Here is the opening to her manifesto poem "I Do":

I do know English.

I do know English for I have something to say about the latest peace stirring between a crack that's split a sidewalk traversing a dusty border melting at noon beneath an impassive sun.

I do know English and, therefore, when hungry, can ask for more than minimum wage, pointing repeatedly at my mouth and yours.

Such a gesture can only mean what it means: I do not want to remain hungry and I am looking at your mouth.

In 2000, the Lannan Foundation in Santa Fe, which sponsors a Readings & Conversations series, brought Li-Young Lee to town. Li-Young read to a packed house, and I include here the ending to his classic poem, "Persimmons," where his father has gone blind:

He raises both hands to touch the cloth,
asks, *Which is this?*

This is persimmons, Father.

Oh, the feel of the wolftail on the silk,
the strength, the tense
precision in the wrist.
I painted them hundreds of times
eyes closed. These I painted blind.
Some things never leave a person:
scent of the hair of one you love,
the texture of persimmons,
in your palm, the ripe weight.

In 2003, in New York, the Asian American Writers' Workshop hosted "Intimacy and Geography: The National Asian American Poetry Festival," and among the many readings and conversations, I remember talking at length with Meena Alexander about literary translation: its impossibility and also its necessity. We talked about translations of the *Mahabharata*, the *Bhagavad Gita*, and the *Kama Sutra*. Meena moved fluidly between languages and cultures, and she ended her poem "Black River, Walled Garden" with this:

The leaves of the rose tree
splinter and flee; the garden
of my childhood returns to the sea.

The piecework of sanity,
the fretwork of desire,
restive bits and pieces edged into place,

satisfies so little.
In dreams come calling
migrant missing selves,

fire in an old man's sleeve,
coiled rosebuds struck from a branch.
Our earthly world slit open.

Around that time, visiting Naropa University, I met Shin Yu Pai, who has a strong connection to the visual arts. Instead of work from that time, I've selected an excerpt from a more recent poem, "Burning Monk," that describes the protest and death of Thich Quang Duc in Saigon:

his body withering
his crown blackening

his flesh charring
his corpse collapsing

his heart refusing to burn
his heart refusing to burn
his heart refusing to burn

As I look back, I see that I met so many Asian American poets in New York. In 2009, the poet and translator Kaveh Bassiri invited me to read in his Triptych Reading series, where he invited three poets to share the stage. I read with Cathy Park Hong and Alison Benis White. Here's a complete short poem of Cathy's, "Elegy":

> Awaken, bull-finch, your noon blink readily. I node ye
> noon-time, noon. Awaken, ye left me slurred, tongue still bobbed,
> robbed of pullet sun, me wig one dread knot
> from sand dune's shoulder, noon
>
> lashed shut, knotted dots dim horizon,
> I ye trebled chill betwixt, if a flood in desert dread,
> ire water's rush, ire swamps gambler's flush,
> I plunge water's surface and look noon,
> look, for the cold meat
> of your hand.

The next stage of this walk involves the importance of translation. Unlike most of my friends, I did not go to graduate school and get an MFA. I learned my craft through translation. At UC Berkeley, I translated the Tang dynasty poets. Over time I reached out to poets of other dynasties, and then, in recent years, with trips to international poetry festivals, I've translated poems into English by contemporary poets in China and Taiwan.

In 2008, Edward Hirsch invited me to edit *Chinese Writers on Writing*. Around this time, I came in contact with Gerald Maa, who, as a graduate student at the University of Maryland, was excited by and translating the important Chinese poet Hai Zi. For the *Chinese Writers on Writing* anthology, Gerald made, I believe, the first translation into English of Hai Zi's essay "The Poet I Most Love— Holderlin." Here are the opening and closing passages:

> There are two types of lyric poets: the first kind of poet loves life, but what he loves is his own self in life; he believes that life is only the endocrine or the synaptic sensations of his self. But the second type of poet loves the vista, loves the landscape, loves the winter horizon at dawn or dusk, what he loves is the spirit in the landscape, the breath of existence in the scenery...

> To become a poet you must love the secrets of mankind, in holy night roaming from one place to the next, love the happiness and suffering of mankind, endure what must be endured, sing what must be sung.

While I consider the stream of translation, it is a good time to reach back to the poems of Angel Island. Two years ago, in her inaugural talk, Kimiko Hahn called these poems the roots and branches of Asian American Poetry. I too have found these poems important to remember as part of our history, and because translations renew their source texts, I've included a recent translation by Jeffrey Leong. His poems don't replace the translations by Him Mark Lai, Genny Lim, and Judy Yung, but they add to the discussion. Here's #40, where a Chinese man incarcerated on Angel Island looks at nature around him. A li is a Chinese mile, about a third of the distance of a Western mile.

> A waterscape like kelp entwined a thousand li,
> The shore path with no bank is difficult to walk.
> Calm breezes enter the heart of the city.
> Such tranquility and joy, who knows I reside in a wooden barrack?

In juxtaposition, I jump cut to Santa Fe, New Mexico, to recover two poems by Japanese Americans incarcerated there during World War II. Most people know about the Japanese American internment camps at Manzanar and Heart Mountain, but few know there was also a small camp in Santa Fe. Through a mutual friend, I met Koichi Okada, who was a graduate student from Tokyo attending Highlands University in Las Vegas, New Mexico. Koichi invited me to read a draft of his thesis, "Forced Acculturation: A Study of Issei in the Santa Fe Internment Camp During World War II," and I was excited to discover three tanka poems by Issei poets. I include two of them here; the first is by Muin Ozaki:

> I stand in line
> morning after morning
> for the cold icy cup
> that pierces
> into my bare hands.

A second tanka is by Keiho Soga:

> Since there is no one
> to kiss here,
> I devour
> one raw onion
> after another.

In addition to these poems, I want to include an excerpt by an overlooked poet, Josephine or Josey Foo, who lives in Farmington, New Mexico, and who works in law for the Navajo/Diné tribe. She collaborated with a dancer, Leah Stein, to create a book-length performance work, *A Lily Lilies*. Here's an excerpt from "View for an Afternoon":

It is a Saturday at the old uranium mine, therefore machines are resting.
They are stripped of their skin.

A dog nearby searches for a heartbeat among the curves and slants, their
interlacing nerves and veins. There is a heartbeat a long way off.

A search in the woods yields bone-like pieces of steel. I throw one –
twenty feet; the dog runs.

There is a hard square, right angles, steps rising no higher than a man,
dark, velvety, vast infinite: interior.

There is stretched weight, a bridge on a hill, gravity, reflection,
and a mirror.

Kundiman, an organization dedicated to fostering Asian American writing,
was founded in 2004 by Joseph Legaspi and Sarah Gambito. I am a member of
the advisory board and have twice served as a faculty member at the Kundiman
retreat that encourages and mentors emerging Asian American writers. In 2015
Joseph and Sarah invited me to share a Saturday evening main-stage reading
at the Associated Writing Programs in Minneapolis with Vijay Seshadri, along
with Tina Chang, who introduced us and moderated our discussion.

I first encountered Tina's work in 1996, when I guest edited the poetry for
an issue of the *Asian Pacific American Journal.* I remember reading through a pile of
submissions, and one poem, "Fish Story," leapt out. I was excited to select it for
publication, and I believe Tina was a graduate student at Columbia University at
that time. Here's the opening:

It is the hour of news. The television cracks
its voice over the radiator and the blue carpet. Always
that same cooked silver of you, oil spilling
from the mouth, ginger and scallions burning

through the scales.

And here's an excerpt from "Imaginary Number," the opening poem to
Vijay Seshadri's celebrated book, *3 Sections*:

Consciousness observes and is appeased.
The soul scrambles across the screes.
The soul,

like the square root of minus 1,
is an impossibility that has its uses.

To come back to Kundiman, Joseph and Sarah have so generously promoted younger emerging poets I want to give their own work some attention. Here's an excerpt from Joseph's leaping one-line stanzas in "Verlaine on the Lower East Side":

I do what you hope to find interesting; you do what I pray is magical.

Our tales twist like tongue-tricked cherry stems.

Face of a fox, heart of a dog.

Are you someone I would buy a bread box with?

This dialogue hopes for more: beyond social codes & rudimental mimicry.

Outside darkened, & taxis circling the thriving, heartbreaking avenues glow.

Corkscrew curl of lemon rind a Möbius strip suspended in vodka.

The twisting forks of my ribs are closing in on my beating liver.

And here is the opening from Sarah's poem, "On How to Use this Book":

You deserve your beautiful life.

Its expectant icicles, the dread forest
that is not our forest.
And yet, we meet there.
The streams streaming through us.
The leaves leaving through us.

Once I was black-haired
and I sat in my country's lap.

So many streams run through the work of Asian American poets today, and I have only pointed out a few of them. In his second letter, Ocean Vuong wrote, "I think writing, to me, is not so much an architecture for closure, but rather, a searching for a myriad existence." I believe the poets I've quoted in this talk are actualizing myriad existence, and this is cause for celebration.

I'd like to close with a trans-Pacific poem I wrote after participating in the 2007 Pamirs Poetry Journey at the Yellow Mountain Poetry Festival in Anhui, China. Some of the Chinese poets who attended included Yang Lian, Xi Chuan, and Yan Li, whose poems I later translated into English. My poem is called "Pig's Heaven Inn," and I add a quick note. A xun is a small ceramic vessel with holes.

By covering and uncovering those holes, set to notes on a pentatonic scale, one can play music.

PIG'S HEAVEN INN

Red chiles in a tilted basket catch sunlight—
we walk past a pile of burning mulberry leaves
into Xidi Village, enter a courtyard, notice
an inkstone, engraved with calligraphy, filled
with water and cassia petals, smell Ming
dynasty redwood panels. As a musician lifts
a small *xun* to his mouth and blows, I see kiwis
hanging from branches above a moon doorway:
a grandmother, once the youngest concubine,
propped in a chair with bandages around
her knees, complains of incessant pain;
someone spits in the street. As a second
musician plucks strings on a zither, pomelos
blacken on branches; a woman peels chestnuts;
two men in a flat-bottomed boat gather
duckweed out of a river. The notes splash,
silvery, onto cobblestone, and my fingers
suddenly ache: during the Cultural Revolution,
my aunt's husband leapt out of a third-story
window; at dawn I mistook the cries of
birds for rain. When the musicians pause,
Yellow Mountain pines sway near Bright
Summit Peak; a pig scuffles behind an enclosure;
someone blows their nose. Traces of the past
are wisps of mulberry smoke rising above
roof tiles; and before we, too, vanish, we hike
to where three trails converge: hundreds
of people are stopped ahead of us, hundreds
come up behind: we form a rivulet of people
funneling down through a chasm in the granite.

WELL-TRAVELED PATH:
An Interview with Arthur Sze, by Esther Belin (2022)

ESTHER BELIN: I am so happy that we have a chance to talk about the IAIA. Thank you for allowing me to have this exclusive interview. When you came out to the Southwest, what were the steps that eventually landed you a job at the Institute of American Indian Arts? I'm interested to hear about how year one turned into year twenty-two. What held you to stay with and develop the creative writing program at the IAIA?

ARTHUR SZE: I moved to Santa Fe in 1972 and worked in the New Mexico Poetry-in-the-Schools program from 1973-83. During that decade, I worked as a visiting poet in public schools all over the state and particularly enjoyed working with Native students. In the late 1970s and early 1980s, Phil Foss, the director of the creative writing program at the Institute of American Indian Arts, periodically invited me to visit his poetry workshop, where I read my poems and responded to student writing. In the spring of 1984, there was a faculty opening, and, along with enthusiastic support from the students, Phil wanted to hire me. At that time, the Institute was part of the Bureau of Indian Affairs (BIA), and I met with the president, Jon Wade. Jon said that there were two major obstacles to bringing me on board. First, the Institute had a hiring policy with preference for Native American applicants, and, second, I did not have a graduate degree; but Jon maneuvered through the BIA bureaucracy and created a position called "Permanent Intermittent." This position did not guarantee, from semester to semester, any classes or benefits. I applied, was hired, and joined Phil Foss and Mei-mei Berssenbrugge as the third creative-writing faculty member. Little did I know that five years later I would become the head of the program.

From 1984-2006 I taught at IAIA and can divide my time there into two segments. From 1984-89, Phil was the director of the program and taught all the poetry workshops. I taught other courses in the curriculum, including Linguistics, Playwriting I, and English Composition II. I had to be creative in my approach, because I had little formal training in those areas. Those years were marked by continual erosion of funding under the BIA, poor management, and low morale. The 1988-89 academic year was the nadir where, after years of budget cuts, the Institute had less than a hundred students and teetered on the brink of extinction. Yet, 1988 was also the year that Congress created a new mandate for the college and pulled the Institute out of the BIA. In the spring of 1989, disgusted by lack of institutional support, Phil resigned. At graduation, I was the only faculty member left in the creative writing program. Although it was a very dark time, I also had a vision of what that two-year junior college Associate of Arts degree program could be.

I talked to the administration and became the new director. Over the following years, I rebuilt the program by hiring faculty, rewriting the curriculum, building a strong visiting writers component, and overseeing the arduous path of expanding the Associate of Arts degree into a full-fledged four-year Bachelor of Fine Arts undergraduate degree program. During those difficult transitional years, I never wavered in my commitment to working with Native students of all ages, from eighteen to eighty, and from so many tribes across the United States. From my very first visits to IAIA, I recognized that the students were remarkably talented and had enormous potential. I was excited at the opportunity to teach at the IAIA, and though I used a lot of my energy as a teacher, I also learned a lot, and that exchange was enriching and kept me committed. By 2005, when I was traveling a lot for my own poetry; it no longer seemed fair to the students to be in class one week and on the road the next. The Creative Writing Faculty at that time included Jon Davis and Evelina Zuni Lucero. In August, I submitted a resignation letter to the dean, Ann Filemyr, and told her I wanted to give the Institute a year to do a proper search for a replacement. Ann responded by saying that I had done so much for the students and the creative writing program that she wouldn't let me leave like that. She petitioned the Board that I be recognized as a professor emeritus, and I left the IAIA with that title in May 2006.

EB: You hit on several significant qualities about the IAIA, most notably that it originated as an Indian boarding school run by the Bureau of Indian Affairs. That history is often unknown and misunderstood. BIA-funded programs generally receive poor oversight and funding, with regular staff turnover. I was a student at the IAIA in the aftermath of BIA control, so I felt the impact of that dark time. I know the frustration from a student level but just hearing your side of the story, I have so much gratitude for you. I need to tell you that the energy you spent and the struggle you endured was worth it for the students. Today, the creative writing program is solid because of your vision. I am a little weepy thinking about how difficult a time it was for you. So thank you. Now let's back up. If you divide your time at the IAIA into two segments, is there anything important in the years from 1984 to 1989 that helped set up the program's later fruition?

AS: During that period, Phil Foss, Mei-mei Berssenbrugge, and I worked well together. After years of publishing student anthologies, Phil was excited about starting an international literary journal, *Tyuonyi,* and Mei-mei and I were two of its contributing editors. Tyuonyi is a Keres word that is the name of the great kiva at Bandelier National Park in New Mexico. It means "the meeting place." Phil envisioned the literary journal as a meeting place for diverse poetries and poetics. In working on the literary journal, Phil and I clarified our own poetics. He also applied successfully to the National Endowment for the Arts for Writers-in-Residence grants. Those funds enabled visiting writers to support the creative writing program through one-week residencies. Some of the poets who came included Ray A. Young Bear, Nathaniel Mackey, and Anne Waldman. After her residency, Anne found financial support at Naropa University to create a scholarship for one IAIA Creative Writing major to attend the Summer Writing Program each summer. Mei-mei was also involved in selecting poets who read at the local Center for Contemporary Arts, and she helped arrange visits by Barbara Guest, Ann Lauterbach, and Michael Palmer, among others. In many ways, those years were crucial seed time. Although I was not consciously thinking about how I could expand and deepen what was there, I knew the program so well that, later, I was able to quickly expand on what was present in nascent form.

EB: Those are giant steps forward to build up a small writing program. Tell me more about what kinds of specific things you did to build the program. How did you expand the visiting writers program?

AS: After I became director of the creative writing program in 1989, I encountered an arduous, zigzag building process. For the 1989-90 academic year, I had only two months to find and hire someone to take the open faculty position. I reached out and hired Jim Sagel, a fiction writer and poet who taught part-time at the University of New Mexico in Los Alamos. He only taught for one year at the IAIA, and then I hired Jon Davis the following year. Together we started to build the creative writing program. Over those years, I drew on my experience from 1984 to 1989 to build a strong visiting writers program, where some writers made a single class visit, while other writers came for a one-week residency that included a reading, two class visits, and hours and hours of individual conferences mentoring creative writing majors. I selected poets who were generous with their time and willing to work very hard at giving feedback to student writing. With support from Lannan Foundation, the visiting writers component grew and, in my opinion, became instrumental to the IAIA creative writing program's success. Some of the poets who came for one-week residencies included Joy Harjo, Leslie Silko, Louise Erdrich, and Sherman Alexie. Other poets who came for individual class visits included N. Scott Momaday, Linda Hogan, Simon Ortiz, Gerald Vizenor, Duane Niatum, Quincy Troupe, Robert

Creeley, Marilyn Chin, and Charles Simic. Jay Wright, John Yau, C.D. Wright, Forrest Gander and many others came for one-week residencies and worked tirelessly day after day doing individual conferences with students. I envisioned these conferences as an opportunity for mentorship, and I believed they were also opportunities for each creative writing student to receive feedback on their budding poetry. The IAIA was a two-year college then, and Gerald, who was teaching at the University of California, Santa Cruz, was a liaison when two students, Irvin Morris and RoseMary Diaz, were accepted and transferred in as juniors at UCSC. At one point Simon Ortiz surprised me by making a significant personal donation to support the visiting writers series, and this component flourished and generated intense excitement among the students. When Lannan Foundation invited me to curate the first year of a Readings & Conversations series at Site Santa Fe, I brought those writers to my classes. Derek Walcott visited my poetry workshop and loved the students. After his visit, Derek shared two important insights: first, in his experience, anthologies of American literature tended to start with Anne Bradstreet, but he believed that those anthologies needed to start with a generous selection of Native American poetry and shift the canon; second, Derek said to me that because the path of a poet was arduous, he always thought there was someone behind the poet who affirmed that poetry was worth doing. For him it was his mother; for me, it was Josephine Miles, when I was a student at the University of California, Berkeley. In many ways, I tried to be that person for beginning poets at the IAIA and pass that gift along.

EB: It's a remarkable group of poets that you brought to the IAIA. I don't know of many undergraduate programs in the country where creative writing students would have an opportunity to meet with and work with such poets. You mentioned Derek Walcott's insight about the program. I wonder what other insights you received from poets about the uniqueness of this program.

AS: All of the visiting poets were impressed by the diversity and depth of life experience the Native students had. I remember Jay Wright said he needed more time than I had allotted to respond to the complexity of the students' work, and he worked tirelessly. John Yau said he thought the students were very talented, and that it was wonderful they were not self-conscious and did not know how good their poetry was.

EB: I think that is still true that there is an untapped reservoir of Indigenous writing and stories. I want to focus now on your teaching experience there. What was your approach, then, to teaching poetry at a Native American [Indian boarding]school?

AS: My approach to teaching at the Institute was to respect students for who they were, to gain their trust, and to inspire them to discover what they could do with language. In the early, precarious days, classes were small, ranging from four to nine students, and I was able to focus on each student. The students had raw, amazing life experiences—some very dark and tragic, some very joyful—and they were able to draw on this depth of experience when they wrote. They frequently did not have the mechanics of writing down, but I prioritized creative exploration in language. In 1989, when I took over the poetry workshop, I realized very quickly that if I told students to just write and bring in poems each week, the results were very disappointing. So I experimented with different approaches. I tried to affirm the importance of approaching poetry with a Native perspective or "spin." I asked students to use, when needed, words from their Native language that were untranslatable into English. I invited students to consider how Native syntax or lack of verb tense could become strengths and not weaknesses to their writing. I emphasized that writing poetry couldn't be taught, but that I could share with them a series of writing prompts that could help them evolve and grow. I also asked many students to put aside their preconception of what a poem might be and to just write with the recognition that words were powerful, that urgency in language mattered.

EB: Yes, I loved the approach of your poetry workshops. The coerced education methods of the BIA were so traumatic. It makes sense that Indian students needed to reconcile their relationship to higher education and figure out how writing could be part of that healing process. I still think about the work that came out of those poetry workshops, those stories. Looking back, you were using a trauma-informed practice before it even had a name. I appreciated that approach very much because as Indian people, we carry intergenerational trauma from federal Indian policies which manifests in many different ways. I wonder how the legacy of the school (in art, fashion, theatre, creative writing) influenced your approach or development of the creative writing program?

AS: Because the Institute had an essential emphasis on the arts and on Native culture, I decided to build the curriculum with that in mind, and I took unexpected approaches. In the beginning, when I had to teach Linguistics, I had to transform that course and make it my own. I developed the class using classical Chinese poetry as the core. For the first six weeks, I introduced students, character by character, to a poem by an ancient Chinese poet. I used poems by Zhang Ji, Li Bai, Wang Wei, Du Fu, Han Shan, and Li He. I not only wrote out each Chinese character but also clusters of words in English under each character. In each class I talked about sound, rhythm, image, and the essentials of poetry. I showed students how the 214 radicals, or root elements, to the language moved from simplicity toward complexity, how Chinese characters embodied juxtaposition, and how a few Chinese characters even incorporated metaphor through juxtaposition. I shared different translations in English of the same Chinese poem, so that students could see variations and also have the original poem with a skeletal translation at hand. The students were excited and began thinking about how the Chinese language connected or didn't connect to their own Native languages, and the class became foundational in furthering their creative process and evolution as poets.

When it came to the larger picture of developing a four-year curriculum, I added in a text/image class, where a creative writing student worked with a student in another discipline or themselves worked in a second genre so that poetry and photography, or poetry and printmaking, for instance, would work hand in hand. And as I developed the BFA degree program, I reversed the normal literature sequencing. Instead of starting literature with a historical perspective by starting with, say, Shakespeare, and then moving forward in time, I did the opposite. I made students start with contemporary literature—contemporary poetry, contemporary fiction, contemporary plays—because I knew that Native students needed, first and foremost, to connect to literary works through intense, immediate experience. After that initial excitement took hold, students were then willing to go back in time and learn from and draw on the tradition. Another important aspect was to foreground Native American literature and make that class foundational and required. And I need to add that I did not do this in isolation. It was a huge group effort. When Kathryn Tijerina became president of the IAIA after the institute separated from the BIA, and funding was greatly enhanced, I was able to hire many new faculty. At one point, the creative writing faculty included Gloria Bird, William S. Yellow Robe Jr., Elizabeth Woody, Barney Bush, Jon Davis, and Julie Shigekuni.

EB: The emphasis on Native American and contemporary literature makes sense. What are some of the unique experiences about teaching at a tribal college?

AS: During my twenty-two years of teaching at IAIA, I probably worked with students from two hundred tribes across the United States. In the beginning, it was very disheartening to see a student from one tribe speak or act belligerently toward a student from another tribe. In those days I especially had to act with deep attention and cultural sensitivity. Over time Native students started to work together and support each other, and their cultural differences became a source of creative energy.

Some of my most exciting teaching experiences happened by surprise in the classroom. I remember one day James Thomas Stevens came into class and said that he thought one of the great mysteries to art was the disparity between "intention" and "effect." Another time I remember Allison Adelle Hedge Coke wrote a poem in Lakota that ended with a line in English, "I knew him well." When I pointed this out, Allison said, "That's interesting. In Lakota I was enacting a farewell ceremony, and when the ceremony was completed, I switched into English without realizing it." When Sherwin Bitsui transferred from a community college in Prescott, Arizona, to the IAIA, he showed me some of his poems and said that his teachers in Arizona were baffled by his work. I took one look and realized that he was describing an out-of-balance world, and I encouraged him to run with it. And there were also unforgettable, painful episodes. I remember one student who shot himself and returned to class after recovering in the hospital. When I asked him what happened, he described a self-loathing where "I had to shoot someone or shoot myself." I mention this latter incident, because it would be easy to glorify Native cultural differences and gloss over difficulties. The IAIA was not a normative college! My experience of working with students at the IAIA was often gritty, and moments of success were hard earned. While an astonishing number of creative writing students have gone on to publish books and are doing well as poets, it's important to recognize that sometimes an unforgettable moment was when a student who had been silent for over two months of class—I was very patient and figured he would start talking when he was ready—suddenly started talking and wouldn't stop.

EB: One of the many reasons I encourage students to attend the IAIA is because of the opportunity to work through those gritty moments with writing. I find that we share similar experiences in regard to moments of knowing and learning from the students. When I went to the IAIA, it was the first time the majority of my classmaters were Native, which created a safe space for me to grow as a writer. For people who are unaware of the Native American experience and the colliding effects of federal policies, the intensity can be overwhelming. It is not a small order to teach in a tribal college. How did your time at the IAIA influence your writing?

AS: My time at IAIA was formative for my own writing as well as for my students. Teaching Native students who had such a range and depth of experience helped me explore and expand my own range as a poet. When I encouraged students to draw on their Native cultures, I dug deep into my own Chinese literary culture. In turning the Linguistics class into The Poetic Image class, I deepened my experience of Chinese poetry by teaching it each year and asking myself what I could write that drew on but was not bound by that tradition. In that class, I also turned to classic Japanese poetry in English translation and used examples of tanka, haiku, haibun, and renku. It took many years, but I have utilized all of those forms in my own poetry.

In addition, specific poems were inspired by students. While teaching there, I tried not to write about any of the students, but, after I left in 2006, I decided to write a long sequence inspired by the IAIA. One of the writing prompts I gave beginning students was to pick a term from an astronomy glossary and use that word or phrase as the title and guiding principle to a poem. I thought of the IAIA as a field of energy, as a star, and as each star in the night sky has its own unique signature of light, I wrote a sequence, in nine sections, "Spectral Line." At the center of that poem, I wrote out a catalog of Native tribes. Each year, at the IAIA graduation, it was customary to say the name of each graduating student and then name their tribe. I thought of students I had had the privilege to work with and, instead of listing their literal names, I substituted the names of their tribes so that the catalog became a roll call. The central section became a spine to the sequence. So my time at IAIA inspired specific poems as well as the evolution of my own poetics.

EB: What are some interesting notables about Indigenous approach to poetics?

AS: There are many notables. The key is for young poets to personalize language and make it their own. In exploring Indigenous approaches to poetry, I believe some fertile areas include the destabilization of norms, where nouns can become verbs, or where sound, rhythm, and syntax are influenced by a Native perspective and subtext. There are overt possibilities in structure, where a poem harnesses naming or enacts a ceremony. These are important approaches that enrich all of contemporary American poetry.

EB: When I look at graduates of the Creative Writing Program, I'm interested in the fact that there are so many and that they do not sound the same. Do you have any thoughts about this?

AS: To the best of my knowledge, there are fourteen former students from the IAIA who have each gone on to publish one or more books of poetry. It's important to point out that this is an undergraduate BFA, not a graduate MFA, program. [The IAIA developed an MFA program in 2013.] If I list everyone's names, including, of course, you, I come up with: Crisosto Apache, Tacey Atsitty, Esther Belin, Sherwin Bitsui, Laura Da', RoseMary Diaz, Santee Frazier, Jennifer Elise Foerster, Allison Adelle Hedge Coke, Layli Long Soldier, dg nanouk okpik, Sarah Ortiz, James Thomas Stevens, and Orlando White. If we include published fiction writers, we need to add Eddie Chuculate and Irvin Morris. If we include playwriting/theater, we need to add Terry Gomez, Cathy Tagnak Rexford, and Kirsten Wilson. Finally, if we include journalism, we need to add Tristan Ahtone and Jason Begay. Oftentimes graduates of a particular creative writing program sound like a writer they studied with, but I am particularly heartened by the fact that these writers do not sound like me. They sound like themselves. And, as I've said, this success was a group effort. In addition to the other creative writing faculty, all of the visiting writers made contributions that enabled this blossoming to happen. I am glad to have contributed to this success.

V • CREATIVE PROCESS

Arthur Sze in Conversation with Tony Leuzzi (2019)

TONY LEUZZI: Congratulations on *Sight Lines*. It's a remarkable book. In one sense, the poems in it are an obvious extension of your previous work. There is your ongoing attention to global matters, the numerous *heres* and *theres* that seem like points of contrast yet are ultimately interconnected. Your language remains crystal clear, with straightforward syntax and grammar frequently braiding disparate matter into a coherent whole. What is more, the poems continue to feel spacious yet full, a balance achieved through careful arrangement of information with masterful formal control. All of these qualities connect *Sight Lines* with your earlier books. However, I have noticed significant changes, too. Whereas previously your juxtapositions often were intentionally jarring, in most of the poems from *Sight Lines* they feel comparatively fluid. This was immediately apparent to me in the opening suite "Water Calligraphy," where you write in section two, "hours were measured / as water rising then spilling from one kettle into another—"; and in section seven you acknowledge that "emotion curves space." This fluidity, which I visualize not as jagged lines but as curvatures—what might account for its frequency in the new poems?

ARTHUR SZE: Thanks for your comments about *Sight Lines*. I agree that the juxtapositions here are more fluid than in my previous work. I think this fluidity has to do with reaching a stage in life that is keenly aware of mortality and transience; it has to do with wanting to be clear-eyed and accepting, even of difficult matters, and to place more attention on continuity and a search for provisional peace, rather than merely highlighting or amplifying breakage. The passage you quote about hours measured as water rising then spilling comes from seeing a clepsydra at work in China, so the continuity or liquidity of time was literal as well as metaphoric. All of the juxtaposed images in that section are images drawn from China, so there's a subliminal recognition that the many pieces, however disparate or dissonant, are part of a single world. The phrase "emotion curves space" has to do with arriving at a stage in life where looking back and looking ahead, where time is short, are charged with emotion. Yeats once used the phrase, "simplification through intensity." In this new work, I have tried to simplify and intensify some of my earlier poetic concerns, and this has, at times, led me to speak more directly.

TL: While we're talking about "Water Calligraphy," I'd like to ask you about section four, where the poem's location is conspicuously various as opposed to singular and centralized:

> Two fawns graze on leaves in a yard—
> as we go up the Pearl Tower, I gaze
> through smog at freighters along the river.
> A thunderstorm gathers: it rains and hails
> on two hikers in the Barrancas: the arroyo
> becomes a torrent, and they crouch for an hour.
> After a pelting storm, you spark into flame
> and draw the wax of the world into light—
> ostrich and emu eggs in a basket by the door,
> the aroma of cumin and pepper in the air.
> In my mouth, a blister forms then disappears.
> At a teak table, with family and friends,
> we eat Dungeness crab, but, as I break
> apart shell and claws, I hear a wounded elk
> shot in the bosque. Canoers ask and receive
> permission to land: they beach a canoe
> with a yellow cedar wreath on the bow
> then catch a bus to the fairgrounds powwow.

Although numerous geographical locales, contrasting emotional states, and the juxtaposition of various moments in time are common in any number of your individual poems, I usually sense a privileged locale or center that unifies the language through a moment of perception or experience in which other perceptions or experiences come together. In this poem, however, I asked myself, "Where is the center?" It was fascinating to see you writing against hierarchy and avoiding the privileging of one space over another. It seemed, in its subtle way, to comment upon these very concerns made manifest in our culture at this moment.

AS: I agree with you that this section of the poem is writing against hierarchy and avoiding privileging one space over another, though the spaces have points of interconnection. On the one hand, the writing against hierarchy can be seen as part of a Taoist or Zen practice of non-attachment; also, maybe more surprising, it can also be seen as an extension of Whitman's fundamental project of democratization and inclusion. And I don't think the one perspective is in conflict with the other—maybe they are even wedded here. In the section you've quoted, one point where different worlds converge occurs when the speaker breaks apart the shell and claws of a Dungeness crab as he sits at a table with family and friends. Instead of an idyllic meal, the speaker finds the act of breakage synchronistically converges with a hunted elk shot in the bosque, and the calm is shaken. Suddenly there's an issue of predator and prey, consumer and consumed, and where does one situate oneself and how does one act responsibly? A potential resolution is suggested in what happens next. Canoers appear, and though they aren't explicitly named as Native Americans, the yellow cedar wreath tied to the bow of the canoe and the canoers who go on to a fairgrounds powwow identify them as Native. And when they ask and receive permission to land, they enact a form of respect and responsibility, humility and reciprocal engagement that we can all benefit from. In this way, these actions stand in sharp contrast and obliquely speak to the tensions of competing claims in our culture at this moment.

TL: One notion that kept returning to me as I read these poems was concurrence. Things that appear or happen simultaneously, either in close contact or across great distances, are relational; often, it appears, inevitably so. Why is this simultaneity so important? What might you be telling us about the world and the ways we live in it?

AS: We live on a planet where many worlds are woven together or are even in collision. Simultaneity is important for several reasons; first, it provides a structure that is nonlinear and allows for the co-existence of different worlds where one world is not necessarily prioritized over another; second, things can happen in close contact or across great distances, but they require close and even arduous attention to understand how the events may be relational. This requires imagination, insight, and understanding. On a small scale, this is what metaphor does: take two things that don't appear to go together and bring them together so that the elements are seen and experienced in a new and deeper way. On a larger scale, we need to understand how these different worlds impinge on, affect, and alter our immediate world. The simultaneity of things is so important because things happening very far away that may at first appear unrelated or unconnected can have a profound and dangerous impact on our lives. I can invoke the butterfly effect of physics to say that modern science confirms this connection, where a butterfly flapping its wings off the coast of the Yucatan can eventually cause a tsunami off the coast of Japan. Like it or not, we live on one planet, and the world's cultures are in constant interaction, drawing from and creating tensions and enrichments with each other. We need to pay close, careful attention to find not superficial resemblances but deep points of connection. And this work is urgent. What we don't understand today in a remote part of the planet can arrive, say, in the form of a virus, and threaten us all tomorrow

[I said this in 2019, before Covid struck**]**, and our actions here and now have profound effects on the farthest reaches of the planet. I can simply invoke climate change to show how we are all living, affecting, and damaging our planet together.

TL: In "Traversal" you write: "between two points, we traverse an infinite set // of paths…". I am reminded of Zeno's paradox about Achilles and the tortoise, where, because the tortoise is given a brief head start, the famed warrior, known for his speed, will never catch up. This paradox is intriguing, even exhilarating, yet horrifying, too: if there is infinite space between two points then there is both unlimited possibility and unbridgeable distance, awe and nightmare. In "Adamant" you write: "you can travel . . . but you can't change the eventual, adamant body." Tantalizing potential and inevitable failure coexist in a powerful way. What does the infinite set of paths between two points mean to you?

AS: It's interesting that you experience the infinite space between two points with simultaneous awe and nightmare. I view the space between more neutrally. The two points, I think, can be "here" and "there," and also the point of birth and the point of death. Because the poem is called "Traversal," I conceived of the two points, on the deeper level, as birth and death, and, in between, each person takes their own path. My intention was to say that each individual moves through life in any number of possible ways, and no one way is necessarily better than another. The effect of what I wrote, that I induced awe and nightmare, interests me. I think there are elements of both in recognizing that it is up to each individual to choose how to live, how to go. And I suppose the disparity between intention and effect here is good: as a writer, I am not trying to confine possible meanings; I am trying to write from my deepest self and discover that the meanings may be manifold and beyond what I intend or see near at hand.

TL: While I definitely see and understand your conception, I was reacting to how various traversals—be they external or internal—are explained. When, in "Adamant," you state that efforts at travel cannot alter "the eventual," the very structure of the language suggests futility or powerlessness. I entirely agree that "each individual moves through life in any number of possible ways"; and I also agree that disparities between intention and effect can be insightful, even fruitful; but the language you use to describe this seems inherently negative insofar as it foregrounds our limitations and failures. To discover "manifold meanings beyond" and traverse spaces between life and death, we must come to terms with being powerless. It seems to me you are suggesting that the acknowledgment of our limitations is an access point to greater perception and understanding, that humility is the precondition to enlightenment.

AS: That's a wonderful reading and response to my poem. "Adamant," is mortality-struck, so there is a strong sense of powerlessness in the face of the inevitable. I agree that our limitations become an access point to greater perception and understanding, and, in a way, that's what the poem enacts when the speaker sees other people, near the end, as "brother" and "sister." And, yes, a necessary precondition to enlightenment is humility. That humility comes from a deep recognition of powerlessness and acceptance that ultimate things can't be changed.

TL: Interspersed throughout *Sight Lines* are untitled one-line poems punctuated at the beginning and the end of each line with dashes. These moments sometimes feel like interludes between longer musical movements. Other times they feel like hinges between the groupings of poems on each side of them. Perhaps they are preludes? Sometimes I sense these one-line utterances are, though separated by longer poems, connected to one another across the book. What would you call these one-line poems? What are their various functions?

AS: I like that you see the untitled one-line poems as interludes, hinges, and preludes. They are all three and even more. As interludes, they rhythmically punctuate the movement of poems in the unfolding of the book. As hinges, they provide shifts of attention or direction. Here I would add that juxtaposition is extremely important. The one-liner, "—During the Cultural Revolution, a boy saw his mother shot by a firing squad—" precedes the idyllic calm of the opening to the next poem, "At dawn you dip oars in water, row out / on a lake," so that the calm of that opening is severely qualified. These one-liners create points of tension and contrast. In addition, they function like a series of non-sequiturs. They come out of nowhere, appear, then disappear, without explanation. A reader is asked to consider how the one-liner may or not have any apparent connection to what has just happened and what is about to happen. The one-liners also function as prelude, because all of the one-liners return in the next-to-last and title poem, "Sight Lines." In that poem, I hope the reader experiences a revelation that these previous one-liners are not gratuitous and that each one is a sight line that helps show what is at stake in the book.

TL: Your poems in *Sight Lines* and elsewhere seem only possible through great discipline. You give extensive attention to the economy and flow of language, rather than spontaneous outpour; similarly, your eye for detail, while often fresh and unexpected, is tempered by what seems meditative detachment. I imagine your work goes through many drafts to ultimately achieve such balance. How distinct are the final versions of your poems from their original drafts? What does the revision process look like for you? Might you offer an illustrative example of what revision looks like for you?

AS: I go through many drafts in writing a poem, and it is indeed a struggle to achieve the right balance. To give an illustrative example of what my process of creation and revision looks like, I've selected a short poem, "Kintsugi." It went through sixty drafts, though sometimes I go through as many as 1one hundred drafts to complete a poem. The fourth draft looks like this:

> he plants spinach and paces along the rows and surveys his field,
>
> he spots a hummingbird nest in a lilac cleft along the driveway,
>
> on a trail, she inhales the aroma of blue spruce,
>
> along the way, a head librarian becomes a parking lot attendant,
>
> he holds an eagle feather in his fingertips,
>
> he can't hear his neighbor's words because so many hummingbirds are at feeders on the porch,
>
> in the early morning, he draws characters in water on slate and watches as the words evaporate,
>
> once women washed out indigo-dyed yarn in this river, but today germanium and gallium particles are carried downstream,
>
> once they built dikes and extended land,

In hindsight, I see that I'm freely associating and don't really know, on any level, where the poem is going or wants to go. Interestingly, the form of one-line stanzas is already there. I wanted a fairly long line and then silence, alternating throughout the poem, so the rhythm was also there early on. When I look at the final version, I see the image of the eagle feather in line 5 becomes "a singer tapped an eagle feather on his shoulders—." The eighth line is roughly complete at this early stage, though it eventually becomes "women washed indigo-dyed yarn in this river, but today gallium and germanium particles are washed downstream—." And the last line in draft 4 becomes "once they dynamited dikes to slow advancing troops—." All the other lines in draft 4 are discarded. The crucial discovery and coalescing metaphor for the poem came in draft 21:

> he surveys his lettuces and paces along the rows—
>
> she inhales the aroma of blue spruce—
>
> eagle feather at his fingertips—

once women washed indigo-dyed yarn in this river, but today gallium and
    germanium particles are washed downstream—

once they dynamited dikes to slow advancing troops—

as a child he was tied to the underbelly of a sheep and escaped marauding
    soldiers—

an apple blossom opens to five petals—

at dawn, he dips a foam brush into a bucket of water and writes *green green,
river bank grass* that evaporates in the sunrise—

as he hikes up a switchback, he remembers undressing her—

he licks salt then downs a shot of tequila—

from the train window, he saw they were cutting fruit off the cacti—

darting out of a crevice, a snake attacked a lizard—

methane rising from a landfill—

picking psilocybin mushrooms and hearing cow bells in the mist—

she likes it when he pulls her to him—

flickering candlelight, flickering eyelids—

he reassembles and repairs the shards of a black bowl with gold lacquer—

red bougainvillea blooming against the glass—

a hummingbird darting from columbine to columbine—

With the repair of a broken black bowl with gold lacquer, the image of *kintsugi*,
golden repair, comes onto the page and becomes the central, guiding movement
to the poem. In the West, we might try to glue the shards of a broken pot back
together and try to disguise, as best we can, that the vessel was ever broken, but
in Japanese culture, a broken pot is glued back together with gold-dusted lac-
quer, and the breakage is highlighted and even honored. In this poem, I began to
feel that a unified narrative (bowl) could be broken apart, and that silence could
be my gold lacquer. With this insight, the revisions of the poem moved steadily
forward—adding, deleting, experimenting with the sequencing—always with
"kintsugi" in mind.

TL: One feature of draft 21 that is markedly different than the fourth is the
presence of dashes. It can be a dramatic, even mysterious form of punctuation.

Because of this, your heavy use of it throughout this poem, and much of *Sight Lines,* is intrinsically interesting; but more than this, your use of it is so supple and various that it begins to take on its own life in the poems. In the opening lines of "Dawn Redwood," perhaps my favorite single poem from the book, the presence of the dash alters what might be ordinarily understood as straightforward phrasing and syntax:

> Early morning light: a young red-tailed hawk
>   glided onto an overhead branch and peered
>
> down at me, but it did not look with your eyes—
>   a battered and rusted pickup lies in the wash;
>
> Navajo tea buds on the trail—I headed back
>   and checked, in the boiler room, the traps,
>
> baited with peanut butter—now a gnat
>   flits against this lit screen: where are you now?

If you had used periods or colons where the dashes are, my understanding of the connections of the phrasing there would be quite different. As it is, I'm wondering how the language on either side of the dash breaks or connects—or breaks and connects—the language on the other side of it. I wonder, too, wherever the dash is the terminal point in a line, if the white space on the other side of it is ultimately the "answer" or "link" to the observation that precedes it. There is so much to think about here, not only because of the lovely flow of images, but because of those dashes. Is this why you so frequently employ this form of punctuation in *Sight Lines?*

AS: Yes, in *Sight Lines*, I am continually experimenting with the possibilities of the dash, and I'm glad you've noticed how I switched from commas in the 4th draft of "Kintsugi" to dashes by the 21st. I think I made that shift in the one-line stanzas because the dashes invested more energy into the momentum of the line. Instead of a standard pause, the lines, with dashes, became filmic, or strobe-like images against white space, against silence. As you suggest, the dashes break or connect or break and connect. I can't always intellectually articulate how each dash functions, but I can say that I was experimenting with small disruptions and leaps, disjunctions and conjunctions, trying to intensify the momentum of the language, using each dash intuitively and musically. As background, I also thought about how Emily Dickinson used dashes in her poems as a rhythmic device and as a form of insistence. I couldn't in any way and didn't want in any way to copy her, but her example suggested to me that I could explore, in my own way, different ways of employing dashes. With that in mind, I agree that when a dash occurs at the end of a line, I'm also considering how the white space on the other side of it may serve as a charged space or link that gives room to pivot. "Dawn Redwood" is infused with loss. It was written in memory of C.D. Wright, and some of the silences that are part of grieving occur in the small spaces where the dashes enact shifts of perspective or momentarily create gaps or pivots of perception. Interestingly, the dashes disappear as a reader moves through the poem—maybe the torque of dashes at the outset subsides into the calmer acceptance represented by commas by the end—and into the final line, which is from C.D.'s poem, "Floating Trees." I can only say this in hindsight; in the white heat of composition, I can't see what I'm doing, I'm just following my visceral instincts.

TL: Many of the poems in the book evoke images that come through senses other than sight. Given this, I was intrigued by the title. Why did you select *Sight Lines?* Did you write the penultimate title poem first, or did you settle on the book title and then create the poem in response to it?

AS: The poem "Sight Lines" was written at the request of Lisa Russ Spaar. Lisa contacted me about an anthology she was editing that related, in any way, to Thomas Jefferson and asked if I would write a poem. At first, I thought I can't write anything "on demand," but then I decided writing about him and his legacy could be an interesting challenge. Living in Santa Fe, I also thought about how New Mexico was outside of America when Thomas Jefferson lived. I did some research and gave myself the invented formal stricture that each line had to pick up a word or words from the previous line (this included the title), and so the structure of the poem was an experiment in repetition and embodied line and circle. I liked how the poem came out, and I thought by taking a bead on America it did something important that I hadn't done before. In the past, I've usually titled my books after long sequences, where the major, title poem is clear. With this short poem, I considered how all the different one-liners were a form—not limited by sight—of sight line. Then, I laid out on the floor all the poems I had written and saw "sight lines" running through so many of the poems: from the evaporating lines of water calligraphy to a single line from CD Wright. As I brooded over where to locate this poem, I came upon the idea of running different one-liners, like preludes or non-sequiturs as we've discussed, from the title poem throughout the manuscript. So I wrote the penultimate title poem before making that the title to the book. Yet, I felt that the title poem shouldn't be the final poem. Bringing all of the previous one-liners together in a final poem felt too much like closure. I decided all of the one-liners coming back together in the title poem were like different slant lines in three-dimensional space converging at a single point: the title poem. The urge to let the lines move through that space and back out in a diverse array led me to write the final poem, "The Glass Constellation."

TL: And then there is another feature of some portions of "The Glass Constellation" and section five of "Water Calligraphy," where certain words or phrases are crossed out, an effect that is quite provocative given that one can see, and therefore read, the words behind the thin single line that has supposedly redacted them. Because of this, two texts emerge simultaneously: the unedited and the edited. I initially wondered if the edited version *should* be privileged over the unedited. But if that were so, why make the original text visible? This dramatizes something else at work. In "The Glass Constellation," for example, words like "pissed" and "fucking" have been crossed out, as if the voice is censoring him or herself. Maybe you want the reader to see this attempt at self-censorship? In the fifth section of "Water Calligraphy" there is a place where you write "smile" and follow it up with "frown"—and then you cross out frown, perhaps trying to strike a more precise or appropriate balance in the line, or because you want the reader to read both versions to decide which is more effective. Could you discuss why you do this in these two poems?

AS: I'd like to give a little background to my use of strike-through lines. I first employed them in a sequence, "The Unfolding Center," that is the last poem in *Compass Rose* (2014). That poem was a collaboration with sculptor Susan York, who also lives in Santa Fe; I wrote a sequence of eleven poems that are accompanied by twenty-two graphite drawings. At an early stage in our collaboration, I was struck by how many layers of graphite Susan made in her abstract drawing, and I liked how the process of drawing was included in the final drawing. I thought about voices in poems and wanted to explore the process of speaking aloud, where the speaker might say something but might regret it or feel that the word or words spoken were not quite accurate. Later, I discovered through a review of *Compass Rose* by Joel Weishaus that I had employed a technique introduced by the philosopher Martin Heidegger. As Joel explains, the use of strike-through lines is called "under erasure," or "sous rature." According to Heidegger, the rationale is: "Since the word is inaccurate, it is crossed out. Since it is necessary, it remains legible." So I arrived at the use of strike-through lines through a very different path, but I concur with Heidegger's idea. Section 5 of "Water Calligraphy" is in a persona, in the voice of someone in China who was tortured during the Cultural Revolution and who is now an older man who goes to a park at sunrise and writes calligraphy, with water, on slate. When people watch what he does and murmur in response, he says, "I smile, frown / fidget, let go," I put a strike-through line through "frown" to show he initially registers that disapproval but then strikes through it because it is, as you suggest, not quite precise or accurate. I wanted to register a tension between what he says and how he responds to it. In "The Glass Constellation," the passage you refer to is in the voice of a man behind on his rent. He is under emotional pressure, and the words "pissed" and "fucking" are spoken but then crossed out because he is conflicted with what he has just said. And, yes, it might be seen as a moment of self-censorship or, more accurately, as the delineation of the tension between his erupting emotion and his desire to contain it. As I've developed voice-driven sections to poems, I've found it helpful to utilize strike-through lines to show more depth and psychological complexity to what is spoken.

TL: We have already discussed the prevalence of distance and traversals in these poems. We have also discussed the simultaneity of oppositional matter or ideas. These poems also draw attention to how our interaction with matter spurs transformation. In the opening section of "Water Calligraphy" you write, "At the bottom of the teacup, // leaves from the character *individual* / and, after a sip, the number eight"; in "Doppler Effect," you state "the more I fingered the clay slab into a bowl / the more misshapen it became"; and in "Courtyard Fire" "as I pull the cord, / spring rips and blooms." Are you suggesting, among other things, our culpability and responsibility to the word?

AS: Absolutely. In this new book, I'm exploring culpability and responsibility to language and to the word. In sipping tea, I noticed how tea leaves settling at the bottom of a cup can move and suggest different Chinese characters. Reading tea leaves is of course a form of divination, so there's also an underlying thematic thread that language is mysterious and miraculous. In "Doppler Effect," you can think of the clay as raw language and how you can overwork language: the more you try to shape it, the more distorted it becomes. In working with language, we have a responsibility to accuracy and to imaginative truth. I can't articulate very well the ending to "Courtyard Fire," which you quote, but the phrasing of that ending has to do with imaginative truth.

TL: You've cited visual art as a point of reference for some of the choices you've made while writing these poems. That doesn't surprise me, as there is a palpable interdisciplinary openness to all of your books. But the art form I most relate to these poems is music; specifically, intricately-patterned instrumental music with an ongoing relaxation and tension of line, music that reiterates and develops certain figures as the movement and progression of phrases unfurl in aural space. I'm thinking, for example, of "First Snow," a poem that beautifully balances shifts from terse, almost tense phrases in present observation to lyrical bursts of language promoted by philosophical reflection. These shifts are so calibrated yet intimate, and they remind me of Bach's "Goldberg Variations." Could you talk a bit about your relationship to music and how it influences—if at all—your composition processes?

AS: My relationship to music is a long one. In elementary and junior high school, I played the piano and then the clarinet, neither with any distinction, but those early years were formative. In 1985, I met the composer Tan Dun, before he became renowned, when he was in China at the Beijing Conservatory of Music. In 1988, when he had moved to New York City, we collaborated on a poetry and music concert work, "The Silk Road," which premiered at the Center for Contemporary Arts in Santa Fe on April 1 and 2, 1989. At that time, Tan used a lot of unusual percussive effects, and he also demonstrated a keen interest in Beijing Opera. I wrote my poem in six sections in couplets with his music in mind, thinking that the white spaces between stanzas would give him space to compose music. The collaboration evolved over months, and Tan Dun created, in the fourth section, a concert inside of the concert piece, which has since been performed as a solo piece. We had the text I wrote for section four translated into Chinese. In performance for that section, Joan La Barbara sang the English; Chen Shi-Zheng sang the Chinese text in Beijing Opera style; Chris Shultis, head of the New Mexico Percussion Ensemble, played rototoms; Yao An played the guzheng, or zither; and Tan Dun played several small *xun*, ancient Chinese ceramic pots set to a pentatonic scale. In the other five sections, I read the lines of my poem in English, and Tan Dun open-endedly choreographed all the musical and vocal lines so that we had to listen to each other during performance to decide when to start and stop. During this collaboration, I thought a lot about tonal shifts, dramatic tension, and ruptures of narrative. I also experienced how important silences were in a live concert. I've taken what I learned through this collaboration into my poetry, and, as you say, the musical possibilities of language have come forward in my new work. In writing sequences, say section two of "Water Calligraphy," I'm keenly aware of the silences between stanzas where I am trying to immerse the reader in a world of charged images. I'm also playing with tonal shifts through careful juxtapositions, and some of these musical effects were learned through my collaborative work with Tan Dun. During the early 1990s, when I was working on my fifth book, *Archipelago*, I listened to a lot of jazz, in particular, Thelonious Monk. His "displaced" accents—they of course are doing exactly what he wants them to do—were important to me as I worked on the title poem and other sequences in that book. I had a lot of fragmented, dissonant passages, and I can't say there was a direct correlation, but I listened and listened to Monk's music and found it inspiring. To jump to *Sight Lines*, in a poem like "First Snow," the lines of the poem are arranged in indented shifting clusters of perception, and consciously harnessing the white spaces on the page helped bring out the musicality of the language. So my interest in music has been ongoing and has informed my evolution as a poet

TL: I had the privilege of interviewing you seven years ago. In that discussion, I asked you about where you, a Chinese American with a global consciousness, see yourself in the tradition of American poetry. A lot has happened in our culture and in our poetry since then, so I'm asking you, in our final exchange, to revisit this question. Has your perception of your place in American poetry changed since then?

AS: When you asked me this question seven years ago, I cited Whitman, Williams, Pound, Stevens and gave supporting reasons why I see myself in that tradition of American poetry. I still see myself in conversation and lineage with those poets, and I'm not sure that my place in American poetry has changed since then. I don't belong to any "school" of poetry or poetics, though, in the last few years, I have to say that I have strong points of connection to ecopoetry. Long before there was a movement in ecopoetics, I believe my thematic concerns of non-hierarchical webs of interconnection, causality-at-a-distance, and letting things be exactly themselves—in 1996, I wrote a sequence, "The String Diamond," that includes, in the third section, a catalog of thirty endangered species, without explanation or commentary—are an inherently ecological position. Furthermore, to represent the interdependence of the human and natural worlds, my use of multiple places to create space that is "constantly relocating, moving, unsettling in such a way that place becomes entangled, destabilized, and decentered" —I quote from an essay by Jenny Morse, "The Ecopoetics of Space in Snyder, Merwin, and Sze"—brings my work into close contact with this movement; though, in the end, we, as artists, shouldn't be concerned about where we fit or don't fit in. I'd like to close with that wonderful quote by Henry James, "We work in the dark—we do what we can—we give what we have. Our doubt is our passion, and our passion is our task. The rest is the madness of art."

"THE WHITE ORCHARD":
Drafts Analysis, Arthur Sze with Eileen Tabios (2021)

EILEEN TABIOS: Arthur, it's a delight to celebrate Asian American Writers' Workshop's 30th anniversary with you by conducting a new poetry-in-progress conversation, as we did for the Asian Pacific American Journal in 1996—an article so momentous it seeded an entire book, *Black Lightning: Poetry-in-Progress*. It seems apt to note the tenure of this historic organization with a still-not-replicated project like *Black Lightning*. For me, the book was special for capturing a moment in time when I was so new to poetry that my questions resulted from an unmediated engagement with your poem we discussed back then, "Archipelago." I'd only paid attention to poetry perhaps a year before we had our first interview. So I recall that as I was questioning you about "Archipelago," I was privately also asking questions about this in-the-wild creature—and blessing—called "poetry." In a way, it was "Archipelago" that persuaded me that poetry was/is a worthwhile companion, then life, to experience.

I stress the "unmediated"-ness of my experience with "Archipelago" because I came to it without any preconceptions about poetry or the poem. I read it simply based on what the poem presented on the page, not on anything about you and poetry in general. In fact, I stumbled across your poem as the title poem for a manuscript sent by your publisher, Copper Canyon Press, to AAWW; the manuscript was a print-out, not yet in book form. And from that "slush pile," *Archipelago* caught my eye. On its own, *Archipelago* was a powerful collection so that even the younger, untutored me was moved to engage with it. I don't know that I can ask such "pure" questions today, because I've since spent two decades with poetry and undoubtedly have formed opinions and hold biases. But I do wish to try again with your newer poem "The White Orchard." Thank you for giving me and AAWW the chance to repeat the *Black Lightning* experience.

ARTHUR SZE: Thank you, Eileen. It is a great pleasure to celebrate the 30th anniversary of the Asian American Writers' Workshop with an in-progress discussion of my recent poem "The White Orchard." As I look back, your book *Black Lightning* was a seminal collection, because it featured the diversity and vitality of Asian American poetry through a personal and wide-open lens.

ET: Before we continue, I'd like to thank the other poets whose generous participation helped bring *Black Lightning* to fruition: Meena Alexander, Indran Amirthanayagam, Mei-mei Berssenbrugge, Luis Cabalquinto, Marilyn Chin,

Sesshu Foster, Jessica Hagedorn, Kimiko Hahn, Garrett Hongo, Li-Young Lee, Timothy Liu, David Mura, John Yau, and (through John's article) Tan Lin.

Let's discuss your poem "The White Orchard."

The White Orchard

Under a supermoon, you gaze into the orchard—

a glass blower shapes a glowing orange mass into a horse—

you step into a space where you once lived—

crushed mica glitters on plastered walls—

a raccoon strolls in moonlight along the top of an adobe wall—

swimming in a pond, we notice a reflected cottonwood on the water—

clang: a deer leaps over the gate—

every fifteen minutes an elephant is shot for its tusks—

you mark a bleached earless lizard against the snowfall of this white page—

the skins of eggplants glistening in a garden—

our bodies glistening by firelight—

though skunks once ravaged corn, our bright moments cannot be ravaged—

sleeping near a canal, you hear lapping waves—

at dawn, waves lapping and the noise of men unloading scallops and shrimp—

no noise of gunshots—

you focus on the branches of hundred-year-old apple trees—

opening the door, we find red and yellow rose petals scattered on our bed—

then light years—

you see pear branches farther in the orchard as the moon rises—

branches bending under the snow of this white page—

ET: I appreciated "The White Orchard" when I read it in your book *The Glass Constellation: New and Collected Poem.* It's notable that "The White Orchard," the title poem for the section of new poems, was included in the 2020 *Pushcart Prize* anthology and also *The Best American Poetry 2019.* But I appreciate "The White Orchard" even more after seeing just about half of the drafts you wrote. The first logical question would be about the poem's impetus and/or inspiration. How did you begin?

AS: I began this poem by listening, looking, and playing with language. I didn't have a particular theme or direction in mind. Instead, I was trying to discover where an image, a musical phrase, a fragment of memory might take me. As I worked through drafts and let phrases emerge out of my consciousness, I started to play with patterns of repetition and created a new form with its own strictures. In this way, the poem that emerged can be seen as an experiment in repetition, musicality, rhythm, and keen attention to silences. If I had to give this invented form a name, I would call it a "Cascade."

I want to point out how the "cascade" formally works. Instead of each line starting with the same word, as in anaphora, I decided to see what would happen if each line, including the title as a line, picked up a word or words from the previous line. So line 1 picks up "orchard" from the title. Line 2 picks up "into" from line 1. Line 3 picks up "into" from line 2. Line 4 picks up "on" inside the word "once" in line 3, etc. Sometimes the single word "a" or "the" is picked up. Sometimes "the" is picked up from inside the word "then." The last line picks up "branches" from the previous line. The title picks up "white" from the last line. The main points of this singular structure are one: to experiment with varying repetition and deepening musicality; two: to employ a structure that embodies line and circle: each line picks up an element from the previous line and moves it forward in a particular direction, but it all circles back to the beginning, so thematically there's the issue of progression and return; and three: to experiment with whether this formal stricture creates some rigor and reveals some underlying necessity to how the language moves, since the poem is not bound by linear narrative.

ET: I'm delighted we can share the news of your poetic invention! And I feel you've named the form quite aptly, given how a reader's response to a single poem also can be a cascade of a variety of feelings. Now, you shared about 41 of the original 88 drafts before the final or published version of "The White Orchard." It's amazing—and wonderful—to compare Draft 1 with the final version, as it shows how "far" your writing process ranged to get to the final draft.

> the hum of a refrigerator,
> incandescent overhead lights,
>
> in the veins of a cottonwood leaf,
> a few pears on branches,
>
> the sound of lapping water,
> men setting squid on ice in the morning market,

While each of Drafts 1 through 17 without doubt can be a stand-alone poem, the drafts also reveal a sense of a gathering of lines with the understanding that they will be subject to future choices as regards inclusion. Is this what was happening with this poem, and perhaps is a general approach given your use of the "list poem" form? I ask in part because these drafts imply an openness to what you may not yet know will unfold, and a welcoming indeed of that uncertainty at the beginning of creating the poem.

AS: Drafts 1 through 17 can be seen as a "gathering of lines," but I would prefer to see them as phrases that rise out of the emptiness of the blank page, as an "emergence" into language. I don't consider "The White Orchard" to be a list poem, even though it's true each monostich has its own integrity and can be viewed as an individual poem. I certainly want to resist knowing too soon where a poem might go or what it will be, and the "openness" you mention is indeed a welcoming of the uncertainty at the beginning of creating the poem.

ET: As I read through your drafts, I came across Draft 7. Here, I sensed that the poem suddenly matured with the second line of the third couplet, "the light-gathering power of your eyes." Do you have some insight/background/opinion to my reaction?

DRAFT 7

> then you are weightless, floating in space,
> methane vaporizes at a low temperature,
>
> the branches of apple trees under a supermoon,
> a singularity,
>
> an atom contains space,
> the light-gathering power of your eyes,
>
> a gap in saturn's rings,
> a positron,

AS: I agree there's a sudden lift or maturation to the gathering momentum of the poem with "the light-gathering power of your eyes." Although that phrase isn't in the final poem, it's almost an admonition to myself to trust what comes into view. And, in hindsight, it's interesting that line 3, "the branches of apple trees under a supermoon," is, in rough form, beginning to take shape as what will eventually become the opening line.

ET: I felt another maturation of the poem with Draft 12. Here, I felt that "connecting of dots" effect with the first and last lines. I felt the poem beginning to reveal muscle for its (completed) self. And the muscle here is epistemological? Any thoughts on my obviously subjective response?

> trust the light-gathering power of your eyes—
>
> under a supermoon, the branches of apple trees gleam in the orchard—
>
> he empties crystals and seeds out of a pouch—
>
> seeds and crystals are set into clusters—
>
> you make a small fire and watch copal smoke—
>
> you do not need to cut your tongue and run a barbed cord through it—
>
> they are standing along a railing while the waters of niagara pour down
> just beyond their reach—
>
> the deafening sound of water will always be there—
>
> a vanishing point marks where a friend has disappeared—
>
> east, south, west, north: which way to go?

AS: That's such an interesting response. In this draft, I feel the connecting of dots between lines 1 and 2: the opening phrase of the poem emerges here, though I can't recognize it yet. Yet the rest of this draft moves in a direction that will not ultimately earn a place in the poem. Lines 3 to 9 move into a specific memory of "a friend" who "has disappeared." The lines here are about Dennis Tedlock, a friend and renowned translator of Mayan texts, including the *Popul Vuh.* Dennis was trained in Mayan divination (line 4), and conversations with him led me to discover the famous image of Lady Xoc, who pulls a barbed cord through her tongue as part of a Mayan bloodletting ceremony. Although none of these lines make it into the final poem, I believe a thematic tension between absence and presence starts to come forward. With one-line stanzas, this draft asserts the rhythm of language and silence, language and silence. In that way, the poem is "beginning to reveal muscle for its (completed) self." The muscle is in part epistemological: What is it we know? How do we know it? But there is also a keen recognition of transience ("vanishing point") that is the emotional force under and behind the language.

ET: The last line of Draft 13 reminds me that I've long thought that luminosity is one of your poetic strengths. But it's not an easy achievement. When it works, the result offers an ease to its surfacing. I feel it as the darkness of text against the page becoming pure light—pure feeling—so that the reader no longer grasps a white page with the dark marks of letters but pure light. I felt this effect with Draft 13:

DRAFT 13

> trust the light-gathering power of your eyes—
>
> under a supermoon, the branches of apple trees gleam in the orchard—
>
> he empties crystals and seeds out of a pouch—
>
> seeds and crystals are set into clusters—
>
> you make a small fire and watch copal smoke—
>
> you do not need to cut your tongue and run a barbed cord through it—
>
> they are standing along a railing while the waters of niagara pour down
>   just beyond their reach—
>
> the deafening sound of water is always there—
>
> a vanishing point marks where a friend has disappeared—
>
> elephant tusks set on fire—
>
> the snowfall of this white page—

AS: Thanks. I believe luminosity has to be earned. If a reader has the sensation of words coming from great depth up into the surface and into light, the poem becomes powerful in this experience. And it's not an easy task to accomplish. At this stage, I'm surprised to see that the ending of the poem is already emerging. I can feel the upward pull into pure feeling and light, but I also want to say that this is only draft 13 out of 88. It is too simplistic to think that the process of writing is simply pulling apples out of the orchard of a blank page. Language can be a thicket and brambles, and I usually have to lose my way in order to find it. Although the poem at the end may appear spontaneous and polished, I have to earn that language through a path that is often thorny, convoluted, and difficult. Here, in nascent form, is that urge toward luminosity and pure feeling, but the poem has a long ways to go.

ET: I love how you describe how language "can be a thicket and brambles" and that you "usually have to lose [your] way in order to find it"! With Draft 18, you introduce the concept of "mono no aware." Was this some turning point in the drafting of the poem? Like some way to unify the variety of your monostichs? Relatedly, was "mono no aware" placed as a first line in the draft as a first thought on what might become the poem's title, and thus inevitably some sense of what the poem will be "about," notwithstanding the difficulty of the term "about" in poetry?

[mono no aware]

trust the light-gathering power of your eyes—

a raccoon walks in moonlight along the top of an adobe wall—

under a supermoon, the branches of pear trees gleam in the orchard—

you hear the clang when a deer leaps over a metal gate—

the snowfall of this white page—

every fifteen minutes an elephant is killed for its tusks—

he recalls the purple skins of eggplants in the garden—

their glistening bodies by firelight—

paper wasp nest layers strewn across the grass—

in the patio, samba music with lights strung along the blooming wisteria—

opening the door, they found their bed sprinkled with rose petals—

near the canal, men lay cuttlefish and scallops on ice—

a glass blower shapes the glowing orange mass into a horse—

AS: "Mono no aware" is an important phrase in Japanese aesthetics. I don't know Japanese, so I can't literally translate it, but I associate the phrase with "the poignancy of things," that there's a keen attention to things as they are, with the simultaneous recognition that they are transient. I put the phrase in brackets at the top of Draft 18 because I was starting to search for the "one" inside the "many." I was starting to ask myself how do these single lines connect: What is the animating force behind the language? What is the underlying emotion? Where is the rigor? In this draft, you can see many phrases that will earn their place in the final poem, and you can also see lines that will be stripped out. In using brackets, I was clearly thinking that the poem would never have this title but that this aesthetic principle might be a singular thread that could help me distinguish which lines were essential and how to start to connect the one-liners.

ET: This is a classic *Black Lightning* question—why did you move the line "a raccoon walks in moonlight along the top of an adobe wall—" from the third line in Draft 18 to the ending line in Draft 21? And how is the switch an example of your thought process on how to rearrange the lines?

DRAFT 21

[mono no aware]

trust the light-gathering power of your eyes—

under a supermoon, the branches of pear trees gleam in the orchard—

you hear the clang when a deer leaps over a metal gate—

the snowfall of this white page—

every fifteen minutes an elephant is killed for its tusks—

sitting in a hot tub, looking up at the stars—

he recalls the purple skins of eggplants in the garden—

their glistening bodies by firelight—

paper wasp nest layers strewn across the grass—

samba music in the patio with lights strung along the blooming wisteria—

they opened the door and found their bed covered in rose petals—

when the pilot soared the helicopter up a ridge and over a canyon—

a raccoon walks in moonlight along the top of an adobe wall—

AS: In Draft 18, the first two lines are reminders to myself, and with the third line, "a raccoon walks ...", I am experimenting with opening the poem with that image. In Draft 21, I am experimenting with ending the poem with that same image. At this stage, I am searching for beginnings and endings and am inside a field of energy. In terms of my decisions as to how to arrange or rearrange the lines of the poem, all I can say is that it is intuitive. I will eventually recognize that the image of the raccoon is important to be in the poem, but I will also decide it doesn't have the imaginative or emotional power to be located at either the beginning or the end.

ET: Why did you delete reference to "mono no aware" with Draft 24? And this deletion also reminds me that you seem to trust the reader a lot. This thought pops up because citing "mono no aware" as a line would be a more didactic line relative to some others. Are you trusting more in resonance and/or the suggestion versus the statement? My rambling question here reminds me that I ask questions that reference narrative content, and yet the matter for you as the poet-author may be more of a poetic strategy/technique/form rather than narrative ... ?

AS: With Draft 24, I deleted "mono no aware" because I no longer needed that kind of reminder to go by. The phrase was helpful up to a point, but now the poem was not bound by that kind of aesthetic vision. There's a full and rich articulation to the phrases now surfacing onto the page, so "mono no aware" was no longer helpful. At this stage, I'm not following a narrative or linear sequence. Instead, I'm pursuing charged fragments and exploring how to mine them and align them.

ET: Draft 25 reveals itself as seven couplets. The obvious question then is what you considered as you switched from couplets to a "list" form or single-line stanzas. I do notice you switch back to the latter as of Draft 29.

AS: In writing a series of monostichs, I don't consider the lines as a kind of

DRAFT 25

> the light-gathering power of your eyes,
> a raccoon walks in moonlight along the top of an adobe wall,
>
> the branches of pear trees gleam in the orchard,
> you hear the clang when a deer leaps over a metal gate,
>
> in the snowfall of this white page,
> every fifteen minutes an elephant is killed for its tusks,
>
> the purple skins of eggplants in the garden,
> opening the door, they find their bed sprinkled with rose petals,
>
> a sparrow perches on a power line,
> he added crushed mica into the mix then plastered the bedroom walls,
>
> you notice that glitter now,
> shreds of a paper wasp nest strewn across the grass,
>
> their glistening bodies by firelight,
> a glass blower shapes the glowing orange mass into a horse,

list because each line is free-floating and has its own autonomy. Each line is a microcosm that I trust will eventually connect to a macrocosm that I can't yet see or understand. In Draft 25, I was exploring whether the lines would have more impact as couplets rather than as monostichs. I was trying to discover if there were connections and urgencies that would be revealed if the poem moved rhythmically in couplet form. By Draft 29, I am feeling that the independence of each line is important, so I shift back to monostichs.

ET: With Draft 29, I see your first use of the em dash; you apply it at the end of each line. So what's the significance of the em dash? Relatedly, when I compare Draft 29 with the final/published version, you add the em dash even to the last line of the poem. What were you thinking about with that choice? What were you thinking about specifically the use of the em dash at the end of the last line? (It reminds me of when I write prose poems and I delete the period at the end of the last sentence as a visual metaphor for the poem's ongoing-ness.)

AS: With Draft 29, I am envisioning the independence of each line, and the use of the em dash at the end of each line affirms the independence and open-ended quality of that line. With that independence, I am also starting to explore the cadence, rhythm, and syntax of each line. And, yes, the last line of the poem also ends in an em dash because the poem does not have any closure.

ET: Draft 30 raises an indented first line "gazing into the orchard." Is this the first or second mention of a title? The final title is "The White Orchard." Please discuss the title's evolution.

under a supermoon, you gaze out into the orchard—

a glass blower shapes a glowing orange mass into a horse—

four thousand miles away, you still hear lapping waves—

you walk into a space where you once lived—

crushed mica glittering on the plastered bedroom walls—

a raccoon strolls in moonlight along the top of an adobe wall—

a great blue heron rises from the pond—

quarrels with a neighbor dissolve at a vanishing point—

you gaze out into an orchard and landscape is autobiography—

you hear a clang when a deer leaps over a gate—

every fifteen minutes an elephant is killed for its tusks—

you save what is precious against the snowfall of this white page—

purple skins of eggplants glisten in a garden—

garden and garner the fruits of your labors—

our bodies glisten by firelight—

though skunks once ravaged corn, the bright moments cannot be ravaged—

you live in the glittering moments but do not show that glitter—

and you know the glitter is foam on a wave and do not love it any less—

someone may find these words years hence and find them curious—

a shrinking cabinet of curiosities whose key is invisible—

it is a singularity unpacked by the human voice

DRAFT 30

gazing into the orchard

under a supermoon, you gaze out into the orchard—

a glass blower shapes a glowing orange mass into a horse—

four thousand miles away, you still hear lapping waves—

you walk into a space where you once lived—

crushed mica glittering on the plastered bedroom walls—

a raccoon strolls in moonlight along the top of an adobe wall—

a great blue heron rises from the pond—

quarrels with a neighbor dissolve at a vanishing point—

you gaze out into an orchard and landscape is autobiography—

you hear a clang when a deer leaps over a gate—

every fifteen minutes an elephant is killed for its tusks—

you save what is precious against the snowfall of this white page—

purple skins of eggplants glisten in a garden—

garden and garner the fruits of your labors—

our bodies glisten by firelight—

though skunks once ravaged corn, the bright moments cannot be ravaged—

you live in the glittering moments but do not show that glitter—

and you know the glitter is foam on a wave and do not love it any less—

someone may find these words years hence and find them curious—

a shrinking cabinet of curiosities whose key is invisible—

it is a singularity unpacked by the human gaze and voice—

AS: Yes, with Draft 30, I am trying out, for the first time, "gazing into the orchard" as a working title. Notice that it embodies the admonition to myself to "trust the light-gathering power of your eyes." At this stage, I've tossed "mono no aware" and am searching for a working title that can help direct the focus and energy of the poem-in-progress.

ET: Elsewhere in Draft 30, we see lines that will end up being deleted, like:

> "landscape is autobiography"

and:

> "a shrinking cabinet of curiosities whose key is invisible—
> It is a singularity unpacked by the human gaze and voice—"

These, to me, are lovely lines; the first can be used easily by others as an epigraph quoted from you. Yet you deleted them, and at this point when I am reading your drafts (since my questions are created from reading the drafts chronologically), I sense a logic to their deletion. That they're more didactic and weigh heavier than other lines. Your thoughts?

AS: Yes, although the lines are interesting in themselves, they are more didactic. I didn't feel the last two lines were helpful, in that the "cabinet of curiosities" leads to the whole genre of collecting and assembling visual works of art, and the "singularity" leads into an astrophysics of time and space. In a way, these issues are implicitly touched on in the poem, but a direct articulation would be heavy-handed. And the first phrase is, as you point out, more potent as an epigraph or as subtext rather than as an overt assertion. Nevertheless, these are phrases worth keeping and might become seeds to another poem. That is one reason why keeping drafts is important: phrases that don't find their way into one poem can be the genesis of another.

ET: I am struck by how you keep drafts. I certainly would keep deleted lines because the lines themselves are lovely. But I'm now thinking that it's this process that might help create a "voice" associated with Arthur Sze's voice which I, as a reader, happen to find recognizable. I also suspect that if this effect as regards "voice" exists, it may not have been something that was of (conscious) concern but something that surfaced after years of your poetic practice. What do you think?

I also belatedly realize that perhaps another reason your poems are so effective is precisely because you consider each line not to be (just) a poetic line but a monostich. As a single-line poem, or poem itself, this facilitates the clearing away of less-than-effective words or phrases within the monostich because the form is so compressed. After years of reading your poems, I'm almost embarrassed not to understand the monostich's significance. Any thoughts on this?

AS: Rather than set aside deleted lines, I like to keep drafts because I don't always know right away which ones might become seeds to new poems. Also, when I go back, if I have the context of a draft, I can catch, as you suggest, a glimmer of voice that helps me recall the emotional nuance of what's at stake. The key phrase or line might be like the tip of an iceberg, and the draft helps me understand the subtext.

In terms of monostichs, I like the compression and intensity that the one-liners afford, and there are different effects that their usage can enact. Sometimes a series of monostichs in a sequence can suspend linear narration and raise issues of simultaneity and synchronicity (acausal meaningful connection); sometimes the monostichs increase the duration of silences and therefore have an essential rhythmic role to play; and sometimes the monostichs, as poems inside of poems, create miniature resonances that aggregate and intensify as the poem unfolds.

ET: With Drafts 65-87, you've compiled your edits from those 23 drafts on one page. It's the only draft presenting your handwritten marks against typescript. I believe many readers will enjoy seeing the poet's marks:

Arthur Sze

The White Orchard

Under a supermoon, you gaze into the orchard—

a glass blower shapes a glowing orange mass into a horse—

you step into a space where you once lived—

crushed mica glitters on plastered bedroom walls—

a raccoon strolls in moonlight along the top of an adobe wall—

swimming in a pond, we notice a reflected cottonwood on the water—

clang: a deer just leapt over the gate—

every fifteen minutes an elephant is shot for its tusks—

you mark a bleached earless lizard against the snowfall of this white page—

(you notice) the skins of eggplants glistening in a garden—

our bodies glistening by firelight—

though skunks once ravaged corn, our bright moments cannot be ravaged—

sleeping near a canal, you cannot forget lapping waves—

at dawn, waves lapping and the noise of men unloading scallops and shrimp—

no noise of gunshots—

you focus on the branches of hundred-year-old apple trees—

opening the door, we find red and yellow rose petals scattered on our bed—

light years since then—

you see pear branches farther in the orchard as the moon rises—

branches bending under the snow of this white page—

ET: Before reading your drafts and our conversation, I read the final version of the poem. So my last questions are based on reading this final version first, and before knowing of your poetic invention of the Cascade.

Firstly, the transition between the first line—"you gaze into the orchard—" is followed by a visually impactful line with the repeated shapes of circles: moon, the "o" of orchard, "blower." Were you thinking of visuality? Because the line is so visual it picks up on the letter "o"s in a number of words and yet you might have been more concerned with sound

Second, I adore the line "clang: a deer leaps over the gate—" because of how it introduces sound, and specifically, a type of sound that wakes up the listener. By inserting "clang" and not just having the line be "a deer leaps over the gate—" I feel you lift the reader (or this reader) off of the page and away from mere memory; here, utilizing the sense of hearing introduces a physicality to experiencing the line that's fresh enough to enhance the physicality of the leaping deer by widening the reader's eyes. Can you discuss the significance of using words like "clang," and perhaps similar such words, as a poetic strategy?

Third, the line "though skunks once ravaged corn, our bright moments cannot be ravaged—" ends with "our bright moments cannot be ravaged." The thought made me pause. Do you believe that—or how do you believe that—"bright moments cannot be ravaged"?

Fourth, I find the combination of these two lines in succession:

opening the door, we find red and yellow rose petals scattered on our bed—

then light years—

to be wondrously romantic, for implications as to how the "we" makes time stand still to the sexiness of prolonged fidelity. I wonder what your thoughts were for this particular combination of lines.

Lastly, I think the ending line is brilliant. "Killer line," as they say. It induces a reflective meta…but really I shouldn't be putting words in your authorial mouth. Please share what you wish about your thoughts as regards (re)turning the poem from worldly experiences to reading.

AS: These are all wonderful observations, and I say "yes" to all of them. In the first and second lines, I am aware of the visual use of "o"s running through those lines, and I am also using the vowel sound of those "o"s to anchor or initiate the opening pulse of the poem. With line 7, I very consciously worked with "clang" to disrupt the flow, awaken, and lift the reader off of the page. And, yes, to the assertion that "bright moments cannot be ravaged." Of course what happens in life can tarnish and ravage us, but the speaker is asserting what Gerard Manley

Hopkins asserted, "There lives the dearest freshness deep down things." I'm glad the line gave you pause, because it's an important moment to consider. And, yes, to the "roses" and "light years." I worked over many drafts to find that very short line "then light years" that affirms the "sexiness of prolonged fidelity." And, finally, you can see how in Draft 13, the nascent "snowfall of this white page" becomes more physical and also how it opens up the meta dimension with the final line, "branches bending under the snow of this white page."

ET: Thank you, Arthur. I'd like to ask you now to compare our discussion today versus what you and I shared through our first *Black Lightning* conversation about twenty-four years ago for your poem "Archipelago."

AS: Years ago when we discussed my poem "Archipelago," I was excited at writing that sequence, and a lot of our discussion went into showing how the different sections coalesced, through juxtaposition, into the ordering of the nine sections. Today, in discussing a single poem, I believe we're delving deeper into the process of writing poetry itself. And I want to thank you for reading my work with such care and insight.

SLEEPERS

A black-chinned hummingbird lands
on a metal wire and rests for five seconds;
for five seconds, a pianist lowers his head
and rests his hands on the keys;

a man bathes where irrigation water
forms a pool before it drains into the river;
a mechanic untwists a plug, and engine oil
drains into a bucket; for five seconds,

I smell peppermint through an open window,
recall where a wild leaf grazed your skin;
here touch comes before sight; holding you,
I recall, across a canal, the sounds of men

laying cuttlefish on ice at first light;
before first light, physical contact,
our hearts beating, patter of female rain
on the roof; as the hummingbird

whirrs out of sight, the gears of a clock
mesh at varying speeds; we hear
a series of ostinato notes and are not tied
to our bodies' weight on earth.

One morning I happened to see a black-chinned hummingbird land on a metal
fence. In flight, hummingbirds may beat their wings fifty times a second, and
to see one stay still seemed like the longest time. I started to play in language,
and the suspense of the still hummingbird led me to the moment when a pianist
lowers his head but does not yet touch the keys. And the lowering motion led
me to the image of a homeless man who bathes in irrigation water where the

water forms a natural pool before it flows into the Santa Fe River. That downward motion also led me to the image of a mechanic draining engine oil out of a car. I mention these details as if they are causally linked. They are not. In writing, I trusted the sound and rhythm, the repeating motion of "for five seconds," and let what happened in my writing happen.

If I write a poem and know where the poem is headed, I find those poems usually don't have deep and essential surprise, and the urgency, that poetry needs. So I often have to shed all notion of what I think the poem wants to say or where it wants to take me. In playing with musical phrases and images, I find a poem can emerge or coalesce without my knowing what it is about. There's a tension between wanting to be in control—I am after all choosing words and shaping the language—and also letting go and being carried into the unknown. In "Sleepers"—I can only say this in hindsight—I notice that the smell of "peppermint through an open window," triggers a memory, then another memory. And in the dark, "touch comes before sight." In this situation, the lovers, though sleeping, are also connected, through physical contact, through an awareness of their hearts beating, and through the sound of a gentle rain on the roof.

The time of the poem takes place in the interval between when the hummingbird lands and when it takes off. And in that space, rather than one space, there are synchronous spaces. Carl Jung once asserted that "synchronicity takes the coincidence of events in space and time as meaning something more than mere chance," and that is what is happening here. In one space, there's a hint of environmental pollution: what will the mechanic do with the used engine oil? Surely he won't dump it down a sewer or pour it into a stream? And gravity, with two meanings, enters the poem with force. Though this poem has a light touch, I hope it has gravitas, a seriousness of purpose and dignity of tone. And, yes, gravity, in its scientific meaning, is an active force. The irrigation water that flows downhill obeys gravity; the engine oil that drains out of the bottom of a car obeys gravity. Yet, when the pianist—obeys gravity and?—finally hits the keyboard with his fingers and starts to play, a series of persistent notes comes out, and that ensuing music somehow affirms that the sleeping lovers are not constrained, like mere objects or weights, to the pull of Earth's gravity. In the way that this poem combines sensuous detail, complexity of experience, and braids the natural, human, and erotic, I believe "Sleepers" is representative of my work at this particular moment.

Finally, just as the gears of a clock have different sizes and speeds but work in unison to track time and move the second, minute, and hour hands of a clock, the different phrases in this poem, some shorter, some longer, work in unison. The poem is linguistically one sentence. There are commas, there are semicolons; each phrase works like the gear of a mysterious clock to reveal the inner workings of emotion and consciousness.

VI · POEMS

AFTER A NEW MOON

Each evening you gaze in the southwest sky
as a crescent extends in argentine light.
When the moon was new, your mind was
desireless, but now both wax to the world.
While your neighbor's field is cleared,
your corner plot is strewn with desiccated
sunflower stalks. You scrutinize the bare
apricot limbs that have never set fruit,
the wisteria that has never blossomed,
and wince, hearing how, at New Year's,
teens bashed in a door and clubbed strangers.
Near a pond, someone kicks a dog out
of a pickup. Each second, a river edged
with ice shifts course. Last summer's
exposed tractor tire is nearly buried
under silt. An owl lifts from a poplar,
while the moon, no, the human mind
moves from brightest bright to darkest dark.

A tea master examines pellets with tweezers,
points to the varying hues, then pushes
the dish aside. At another shop, a woman
rinses a cylindrical cup with black tea:
we inhale, nod, sip from a second cup—
rabbit tracks in snow become tracks
in my mind. At a banquet, eating something
sausage-like, I'm told, "It's a chicken's ball."
Two horses huddle under leafless poplars.
A neighbor runs water into an oval container,
but, in a day, the roan bangs it with his hoof.
The skunks and raccoons have vanished.
What happened to the End World Hunger project?
Revolutionary slogans sandblasted off
Anhui walls left faint outlines. When
wind swayed the fragrant pine branches
in a Taiwan garden, Sylvie winced, "Kamikaze
pilots drank and whored their last nights here."

SPECTRAL LINE

I

Who passes through the gates of the four directions?
Robin coughs as she tightens a girth, adjusts saddle,
and, leading Paparazzo past three stalls, becomes
woman-leading-horse-into-daylight. Though the Chu
army conquered, how long does a victory last?
The mind sets sliver to sliver to comprehend, spark;
the mind tessellates to bring into being a new shape.
When the Blackfoot architect unveiled his master plan
with a spirit way leading to a center that opened
to the four directions, I saw the approach to
the Ming Tombs, with pairs of seated then standing
lions, camels, elephants, horses lining the way.
I snapped when, through the camera lens,
I spotted blue sneakers—but not the woman—protruding
from the sides of a seated horse, and snapped
a white-haired woman with bound feet munching fry bread.
Peripheral details brighten like mating fireflies.
Then Gloria pointed to the east, gasped,
"Navajos will never set foot here: you've placed
these buildings in the ceremonial form of a rattlesnake."

Blinking red light on the machine: he presses
the button, and a voice staggers, "I'm back,"

"I don't know where I am," "I drive but can't
recollect how I get to where I am,"—whiteout

when a narwhal sprays out its blowhole and water
crystallizes in air—"thirty-three days."

He presses replay: the voice spirals, "I lost
four members of my family in a whaling accident";

he writes down numbers, 424-0590, dials,
"My cousin killed himself after his girlfriend

killed herself" richochets in his ears; though
the name is blurred, he guesses at bowhead

ribs in a backyard, canisters of radioactive
waste stored inland on Saint Lawrence Island;

twenty below: Yupik children play string games;
when he broke the seal on a jar of smoked

king salmon, he recalled his skin and clothes
reeked of smoke from the float-house woodstove.

3

The stillness of heart-shaped leaves breaks
when a grasshopper leaps. I have never
watched so many inch along branches before.
Though they have devastated butterfly bushes,
they have left these lilacs unscathed, but can I
shrug, be marathoner-running-into-spring-light-
over-piñon-dotted-hills? The mind may snag,
still, weigh, sift, incubate, unbalance,
spark, rebalance, mend, release; when one
neighbor cuts grasses infested with grasshoppers,
inadvertently drives them into another's
organic farm loaded with beets, lettuce, basil,
carrots, kale, chard: we cannot act as if
we were asleep, do not entrench boundaries
but work to dissolve them. From light to dark
is a pass of how many miles? Together they sowed
dark millet and reclaimed the reed marsh.
As we entwine in darkness-beginning-to-trace-
light, dew evaporates off tips of grasses.

4

North they headed to Water Bend, what joy awaited them?

"I had to shoot myself or shoot someone else";

cries of snow geese in the wave of sunrise;

the secretary winked, "I'm wearing edible panties";

concubines were immolated on the emperor's death;

the green tips of a leafing apple;

"Here are instructions for when I am dead";

he was retracing the Long Walk;

when we addressed them as *tongzhi*, comrades, they laughed;

she swallowed the white sleeping pills and nearly OD'd;

the spring wind blew the ax off the chopping block;

when confronted with plagiarized lines, he shrugged, "I dreamed them";

the ex-marine checked staff desks at 8:20 for attendance;

from the south, elephants; from the west, horses; from the north, camels;

stepping through the miniature garden, they had no idea
they were writing the character *heart*;

she danced in a topless bar;

when the army recruiting film previewed in the underground bomb shelter,
the crowd jeered;

she surprised him with a jar of Labrador leaves;

"Try to add to the sum total of human culture";

though the edges and angles are many, who knows their number?

5

Acoma Pueblo,
Diné,
Crow,
Oglala Lakota,
Menominee,
Northern Ute,
Zuni Pueblo,
Kiowa,
Muckleshoot,
Standing Rock Lakota,
Muscogee,
Ojibwe,
San Ildefonso Pueblo,
Comanche,
Tlingit,
Mescalero Apache,
Siberian Yupik,
Jemez Pueblo,
Pawnee,
Chugach/Alutiiq,
Mohawk,
Swampy Cree,
Osage,
Taos Pueblo,
Arapaho,
Jicarilla Apache,
Paiute,
Haida,
Onandaga,
Cochiti Pueblo,
Sioux,
Eastern Shawnee,
Caddo,
Santa Clara Pueblo,
Northern Cheyenne,
Prairie Band Potawatomi,
Choctaw,
Chickasaw,
Tsalagi,
Inupiat.

6

We forage for black and yellow morels
under tulip poplars, but they are camouflaged
on the forest floor. Wherever I squint,
I mark varicolored leaves, clusters of deer scat;
at first I zigzag a branch back and forth
under leaves, expecting to uncover some,
then learn to spot-check near the trunks,
forage farther out above the roots among
lichened rocks. We bring two dozen back,
sauté them, add to pasta, salad; sip wine;
but what coalesces in the body for weeks
are glimpses of blossoming redbuds while
driving along a road; horses by the second gate;
lights on the porch; a basket of apples,
bread, farm milk set at a downstairs table;
rocking horse upstairs; two tapers lit;
quicksilver kisses, a diamond light; and,
before, tremor when you felt something odd:
pulled a black tick off from behind your ear,
brushed a smaller one out of your hair.

7

Who rescues hunters tipped into arctic waters?
The hour is a cashmere scarf; as a Black man

near a fountain raises saxophone to his lips
and showers the street with shimmering gold,

red lights of an ambulance weaving in traffic
bob into distance. From a dome, a pendulum

swings, almost touches numbers that mark
the hours in a circle on the floor. When

Robin's coworkers were terminated, she left
her telecommunications job to groom the horses

she loves, even in zero-degree weather; she
cinches a saddle on Nemo even now. A meadow

mushroom, covered overnight under a glass bowl,
releases, onto white paper, a galaxy of

chocolate-brown spores. When you are still,
you spot the chance tracks of the living.

Who can suspend time on a string, make it
arc back and forth while earth rotates around it?

8

Incoming freshmen have been taken hostage,
the letter to the president began; we demand
computers and art supplies; limo service
to the Gathering of Nations; the sum total
of Pell Funds be released at once. Benildus Hall
is our headquarters. When the SWAT team
surrounded the building, someone pointed
to the small print: "Happy April First."
The mind seizes a spore then releases it.
Descending into the Ming Tomb, I discerned
electric lights; a cold, iron railing;
people shuffling down stairs; camera flashes;
people shuffling across, up the other side,
then out; but nothing was at the center;
only now—the moment when water from six
directions is water from the six directions.
A neighbor listens for wings before dawn;
plums begin to begin to drop from branches.

9

"A driver's door opened, and a head rolled
out of the burning car"—once she told me,

I could not expunge it. A backhoe beeps
when the driver moves it into reverse, beeps

above the din of morning traffic. A ginkgo
flames into yellow-gold, while, elsewhere,

red tulips flare on a slope. The mind weighs,
balances antinomies: at graduation, a student

speaker carries a black bag to the podium,
unveils bow, arrows, his entire body shaking,

and threatens to take aim at board members—
dissolves into air; a student in the audience

who slurs "far out" after every sentence
dissolves into air; the man who wafts eagle

feather above head, shoulders, along arms,
onto palms—dissolves into air; singers and

drummers who start and end dissolve into air;
and stillness, as we stir to dawn light, breaks.

DIDYMA

I

Disoriented, a woman wanders in the riverbed
east then west then east, asks us how to get
to County Road 101G. We stare at vertebrae
and long bones that protrude out of her plastic bag,
discern how one day the scavenger will become
the scavenged. At thirteen you dipped leaves
into melted wax in an aluminum pan on a stove,
had an inkling that in order to seal the shapes
you had to asphyxiate the leaves. And as
the area of your knowledge grew, the circumference
of your ignorance was always increased. You had
no idea you would live to recall so many deaths,
that they would become spots along a Pacific
coastline where you would come to gather salt.
You yearn for the ocean spray to quicken your eyes,
yearn for the woman you love to sway and rock.
When she sways and rocks, you sway and rock;
when you sway and rock, she sways and rocks;
when you convulse together, it is not hallucinatory
but a splendor that scavenges days and nights.

The shortest distance between two points is a straight line;

"Slob!"

red salamanders spawned in the Tesuque River;

an ocelot placed a paw on his chest while he slept;

he slapped a mosquito between his hands;

the position of beads on the abacus represented nyctalopia;

asphyxiated in a hotel room;

water in the black rubber bucket froze and never thawed;

red-winged blackbirds congregate in the cattails;

when he closed his eyes, she was there;
when he opened his eyes, she was there;

was afraid to cut the deck;

mosquito larvae quiver the water in the barrel;

rubbed her nipples;

sighted a rhinoceros in the crosshairs and went blind;

rearranged a tangram into the shape of a butterfly;

when he took off his glasses,
oncoming headlights became volvox floating on black water;

slashed the waves with ten thousand whips;

sunlight erased blue thumbprints but left the graphite lines unscathed;

"The earth rests upon water."

3

What can be described can happen, he thought,
and visualized an ice cube sliding through a cup,
water passing through two slits in a wall:
quantum mechanics in the ensuing pattern of waves.
An hour after they ingested psilocybin mushrooms,
he lifted a cantaloupe in the garden, beheld
its weight, started at the intricate fretwork
on its skin; she touched a peach leaf, recalled
when she wrapped the first peach in white cheesecloth,
the juice on their fingers as they each ate half.
She pinched off tips of budding basil plants
and savored the aroma under her fingernails;
a heron landed near the top of a cottonwood,
but though he half expected a cry none came.
They poured and rubbed oil onto each other's skin;
their sighs and groans made the air tremble,
roil. They erased the plum bruises of a day,
restored themselves at a still point in the waves.

4

Green tomatoes on the windowsill:
if they are exposed to sunlight, will they ripen?

thud: a sparrow flies into kitchen glass;

they planted tulips on the slope behind the kitchen;

"Punks!"

he liked the digging;
she liked the slight weight of a bulb in her hand;

patter of rain on skylight;

they would forget the precise locations
but be surprised in spring;

at the Stop sign,
who slowed and hurled a rock through the window?

as simple as a wavelength;

slivers of glass on the sofa, pillows, rug;

it is impossible to know precisely the velocity and position;

by the time you know the brightest yellow of a cottonwood leaf,
it's somewhere else;

yellow hawthorn leaves on the walkway;

shiver, shiver, shiver, shiver, shiver;

who walked from Miletus to Didyma?

he closed and opened his eyelashes along her ear.

5

A point of exhaustion can become a point of renewal:
it might happen as you observe a magpie on a branch,
or when you tug at a knot and discover that a grief
disentangles, dissolves into air. Renewal is not
possible to a calligrapher who simultaneously
draws characters with a brush in each hand;
it occurs when the tip of a brush slips yet swerves
into flame. A woman offers jasmine, dragonwell,
oolong teas: I inhale the fragrances, sip each one,
see chickens in stacked cages, turtles in tanks.
A man hosed blood off speckled white floor tiles
as we zigzagged toward the restaurant; over lunch,
I thought I heard moans and shrieks; when we left,
I glimpsed two white rabbits hauled by their necks
to a chopping block. The glint of the momentary
might dissolve like snow on water, or it might
burst into flame: yellow incense sticks smoking
in a cauldron, a large thin jasper disk that glows
like a harvest moon, the warmth in a glassed garden,
the way our daughter likes to rub foreheads.

6

Cr-rack! She stopped sewing when she heard the rock
shiver the glass window into shards, then the car
revved and sped up County Road 84 into darkness.
The moments you are disoriented are moments
when ink splatters onto the fibers of white paper.
As the area of your ignorance grows, it is possible
the circumference of your knowledge is increased.
Months after a brain aneurysm, when a man whispers
to his wife, "Nothing you do can ever make me happy,"
she turns to the midnight and sobs. When Xerxes
ordered his army to slash the waves of the Hellespont,
he slashed his own fingers to the tendons. Today
we gaze across the Dardanelles—whitecaps on teal water,
a few freighters zigzag down from the Black Sea.
Sunlight flares at the edges of leaves; heat ripples
up from the noon street and from rusted car tops.
The salt in the air stings my eyes: I lift a latch,
step into a patio: bird-of-paradise in bloom;
but, approaching the window, I find peeled paint,
cobwebs; it's dingy inside. I turn, wade into sleep.

"Do-as-you're-told scum sucker, you're the reason there are hydrogen bombs,"
yelled at the postal worker
behind the counter—

it leopards the body—

cringes at strangled
anteaters and raccoons hanging in the market—

it leopards the body—

wakes to pulverized starfish in his shoes—

it leopards the body—

disinterred a man and woman
sealed for 1,855 years
under jade plaques stitched with gold thread—

it leopards the body—

winced at hundreds of cicadas stridulating in the umbrella pines—

it leopards the body—

placed a blackbird with a red gash in the trash bin—

it leopards the body—

catches lamb shank in the smoke—

it leopards the body—

recovers a red tulip from inside a corkscrew dream—

it leopards the body—

combusts when they candlelight touch—

it leopards the body—

cars clunk
as they drive off the ferry at Çanakkale.

8

You walk up the steps and find a double peristyle
with a deep entrance porch filled with columns;
at the base of the columns is an octagonal set
of carved dragons, mermaids, and palmettes.
You turn, stride down a dark and narrow vaulted ramp
that emerges with blinding light into a large hall
open to the sky; a continuous frieze on three walls
has a central acanthus flanked by griffins and lyres.
At the far end, roped off by string, is the foundation
of an inner temple with steps that drop to a spring;
when you walk toward this sanctum and look back,
you see stairs to the platform of epiphanies at the rear.
You gaze up to the top of a sixty-five-foot column,
step up to the cord but can't get near enough
to see if the spring is dry or wet. You hunger
for insight into the precarious nature of becoming,
gaze at the woman you love, whet at how passion
is water from a spring, realize that yesterday,
exhausted, you were not going to come this far,
but today, having come, you have sunlight in your hands.

9

Because one stirred the entrails of a goat immolated on an altar,

because a magpie flicks tail feathers,

because blush-red tulips bloomed on the walkway,

because one speaks without fear of reprisal,

because a man—crushed in the debris of aluminum doors, steering wheel,
    dashboard, shivered windshield—bleeds and moans,

because he had to visualize black petunias in order to spot Black Trumpets
    on the forest floor,

because he slowly bites the back of her neck,

because an eagle glides over the courtyard with outstretched wings,

because a woman fasted, chewed laurel leaves, swayed in noon heat,
    stammered *the here is always beginning*;

because she brushes her hair across his eyelids,

because bells tinkle around the necks of goats,

because the ruins of this moment are chalk-white dust in your hands,

because a grain of sand lodged,

because loss is a seed that germinates into *all things are full of gods*,

because a circle opens in all directions,

10

nine purple irises bloom in a triangular glass vase—

a pearl forms in an oyster—

she folds a prayer and ties it to a green cryptomeria branch—

threaded sponges are hanging in the doorway—

a slug crawls along a railroad tie—

a double bass upstairs suffused the house with longing—

silk tree leaflets fold up when touched—

waking out of her coma, she vowed, "I will dip my hands in ink and drag
    them across white mulberry paper"—

a hummingbird, sipping at a columbine, darted off—

red mullets thrash in the water—

one casts to the end of time—

she wore gold-hooped earrings with her black dress—

urn shards were incorporated into the stone walls of houses—

they swam in the Aegean—

blossoming yellow forsythia is the form and pressure of the hour.

"Acequias as Quipus, Quipus as Poems" appeared in *Water's Edge: Writing on Water*, edited by Lenore Manderson and Forrest Gander. Copyright ©2023 by Northwestern University, Published 2023 by Curbstone Books/Northwestern University Press. All rights reserved. This essay also appeared in *Conjunctions.*

"An Interview with Arthur Sze," by Eric Elshtain, appeared in *Chicago Review,* 50:2/3/4: Winter 2005.

Arthur Sze, "After a New Moon," "First Snow," "Didyma," "Pig's Heaven Inn," "Quipu" (section I only)," "Red Breath," "Returning to Northern New Mexico After a Trip to Asia," "Sight Lines," "Sleepers," "Spectral Line," and "The White Orchard" from *The Glass Constellation: New and Collected Poems.* Copyright © 2021 by Arthur Sze. Reprinted with the permission of The Permissions Company, LLC, on behalf of the author and Copper Canyon Press.

"Sight Lines: Arthur Sze in Conversation with Tony Leuzzi" appeared in *The Brooklyn Rail* (October 2019).

"Demolishing Hierarchy" appeared in *Kenyon Review Online;* subsequently in *Talk Poetry: Poems and Interviews with Nine American Poets*, ed. David Baker (University of Arkansas, 2012).

Ma Chih-Yüan, "Autumn Thoughts," from *The Silk Dragon: Translations from the Chinese* by Arthur Sze. Translation copyright © 2001 by Arthur Sze. Reprinted with the permission of The Permissions Company, LLC, on behalf of Copper Canyon Press.

"On Sleepers" appeared in *Personal Best: Makers on their Poems that Matter Most,* ed. Erin Belieu and Carl Phillips (Copper Canyon Press, 2023).

"Polysemous Poetry: An Interview with Arthur Sze" appeared in *Passwords Primeval*, ed. Tony Leuzzi (BOA Editions, 2012).

"Revealing and Reveling in Complexity" appeared in *On Becoming a Poet,* ed. Susan Terris (Marsh Hawk Press Inc., 2022).

"The Streams Streaming Through Us: The Rich Diversity of Asian American Poetry" appeared in *The Asian American Literary Review,* vol II.

"Well-Traveled Path: An Interview with Arthur Sze," by Esther Belin, appeared in *Poetry,* 2022.

"The White Orchard," Drafts Analysis with Eileen Tabios appeared in *The Margins*, Asian American Writers Workshop, 2021.

In "The Streams Streaming Through Us," the following poems, with specific permissions, were quoted:

Meena Alexander, excerpt from "Black River, Walled Garden." In *Illiterate Heart: Poems*. Copyright © 2002 by Meena Alexander. Published 2002 by TriQuarterly Books/Northwestern University Press. All rights reserved.

"Rhapsody in Plain Yellow," from *Rhapsody in Plain Yellow*, by Marilyn Chin. Copyright © 2002 by Marilyn Chin. Used by permission of W. W. Norton & Company, Inc.

"Elegy," from *Dance Dance Revolution*, by Cathy Park Hong. Copyright © 2007 by Cathy Park Hong. Used by permission of W.W. Norton & Company, Inc.

"O-Bon: Dance for the Dead," from *River of Heaven*, by Garrett Hongo, copyright © 1988 by Garrett Hongo. Used by permission of Alfred A. Knopf, an imprint of the Knopf Doubleday Publishing Group, a division of Penguin Random House LLC. All rights reserved.

Li-Young Lee, excerpt from "Persimmons," from *Rose*. Copyright © 1986 by Li-Young Lee. Reprinted with the permission of The Permissions Company, LLC, on behalf of BOA Editions Ltd.

Joseph O. Legaspi, excerpt from "Valentine on the Lower East Side," from *Threshold*. Copyright © 2017 by Joseph O. Legaspi. Reprinted with the permission of The Permissions Company, LLC, of behalf of CavanKerry Press,

Vijay Seshadri, "Imaginary Number," from *3 Sections*. Copyright © 2013 by Vijay Seshadri. Reprinted with the permission of The Permissions Company, LLC on behalf of Graywolf Press, graywolfpress.org.

Ocean Vuong quotes appeared in the *Asian American Literary Review*, vol. 11.

All other quotes appeared with permission of the poets quoted.

I want to thank all of the poets and editors who made this book of interviews and essays possible: David Baker, Erin Belieu, Esther Belin, Lawrence-Minh Bùi Davis, Eric Elshtain, Forrest Gander, Dana Isokawa, Tony Leuzzi, Gerald Maa, Lenore Manderson, Bradford Morrow, Jim Natal, Jenna Peng, Carl Phillips, Eileen Tabios, and Susan Terris. I also thank Anna Gallegos, Kate O'Donnell, Mary Wachs, and David Skolkin for their editorial acumen, copy-editing, design, and support.

DAVID BAKER is the author of twelve books of poetry, including *Whale Fall* and *Swift: New and Selected Poems.* The poetry editor of *The Kenyon Review* for over twenty-five years, he currently edits the "Nature's Nature" series for *Kenyon Review.*

ESTHER G. BELIN is a Navajo Nation citizen who teaches in the Native American and Indigenous Studies department at Fort Lewis College and is a poetry faculty mentor in the Institute of American Indian Arts Creative Writing MFA program. She is the author of two collections of poetry: *Of Cartography*, and *From the Belly of My Beauty*, winner of the 2000 American Book Award; and is one of four editors of *The Diné Reader: An Anthology of Navajo Literature*, winner of the 2022 American Book Award.

ERIC ELSHTAIN is poet-in-residence at the Field Museum in Chicago.

TONY LEUZZI is a poet, critic, and art maker whose books include *Fog Notes* and *Meditation Archipelago.* He is a regular contributor to *The Brooklyn Rail.*

JIM NATAL is the author of three books of lyric poems: *Memory and Rain, Talking Back to the Rocks,* and *In the Bee Trees,* as well as two collections written in contemporary haibun form: *52 Views: The Haibun Variations,* and *Spare Room.* He is the co-founder of Conflux Press

EILEEN R. TABIOS has released over seventy collections of poetry, fiction, essays, and experimental biographies, including *Because I Love You, I Become War.* She is also the founding editor of the online publication *The Halo-Halo Review.*

ARTHUR SZE is a poet, translator, and editor who has lived in New Mexico over fifty years. He is the author of twelve books of poetry, including *Into the Hush* (Copper Canyon Press, 2025), *The Glass Constellation: New and Collected Poems* (Copper Canyon Press, 2021), selected for a 2024 National Book Foundation Science + Literature Award; *Sight Lines* (2019), which received the National Book Award for Poetry; *Compass Rose* (2014), a Pulitzer Prize finalist; *The Ginkgo Light* (2009), selected for the PEN Southwest Book Award and the Mountains & Plains Independent Booksellers Association Book Award; *Quipu* (2005); *The Redshifting Web: Poems 1970–1998* (1998), selected for the Balcones Poetry Prize and the Asian American Literary Award; and *Archipelago* (1995), selected for an American Book Award. He has also published *The Silk Dragon II: Translations of Chinese Poetry* (Copper Canyon Press, 2024) and edited *Chinese Writers on Writing* (Trinity University Press, 2010).

A recipient of the 2024 Rebekah Johnson Bobbitt National Prize for Poetry, a Ruth Lilly Poetry Prize, the Shelley Memorial Award, the Jackson Poetry Prize, a Lannan Literary Award, a Guggenheim Fellowship, a Lila Wallace-Reader's Digest Writers' Award, two National Endowment for the Arts Creative Writing Fellowships, a Howard Foundation Fellowship, as well as five grants from the Witter Bynner Foundation for Poetry, Sze was the first poet laureate of Santa Fe, New Mexico. His poems have been published in *The American Poetry Review, The Atlantic, Best American Poetry, Boston Review, Conjunctions, Harper's Magazine, Harvard Review, The Kenyon Review, The Nation, The New Republic, The New York Review of Books, The New York Times, The New Yorker, The Paris Review, Poetry, The Yale Review* and Pushcart Prize anthologies. His work has been translated into fifteen languages, and he has read his poetry internationally in Beijing, Cardiff, Delhi, Havana, Hong Kong, London, Medellín, Paris, Rotterdam, Taipei, and Vilnius. *The Glass Constellation: New and Selected Poems,* translated by Diana Shi, with a foreword by George O'Connell, was published in Chinese (Guangxi Normal University Press, 2023). A Portuguese edition of *Sight Lines, Linhas Horizontes,* translated by Júlio Antonio Bonatti Santos, with a preface by Luis Marcio Silva, was published in São Paulo, Brazil (Piparote, 2024). A Chancellor Emeritus of the Academy of American Poets and a fellow of the American Academy of Arts and Sciences, Arthur Sze is a professor emeritus at the Institute of American Indian Arts.

Project direction: Anna Gallegos
Editorial: Mary Wachs, Kate O'Donnell
Design and Production: David Skolkin
Manufactured in the United States of America
10 9 8 7 6 5 4 3 2 1

Library of Congress Cataloging-in-Publication
Names: Sze, Arthur, author.
Title: The white orchard : selected interviews, essays, and poems / Arthur Sze.
Description: Santa Fe : Museum of New Mexico Press, 2025. | Includes bibliographical references.
Identifiers: LCCN 2024049537 (print) | LCCN 2024049538 (ebook) | ISBN 9780890136904 (hardcover) | ISBN 9780890136911 (ebook)
Subjects: LCSH: Creation (Literary, artistic, etc.) | Poetry—Authorship. | LCGFT: Interviews. | Essays. | Poetry.
Classification: LCC PS3569.Z38 W45 2025 (print) | LCC PS3569.Z38 (ebook) | DDC 818/.5409 [B]--dc23/eng/20241115
LC record available at https://lccn.loc.gov/2024049537
LC ebook record available at https://lccn.loc.gov/2024049538

ISBN: 978-089013-690-4

Museum of New Mexico Press
PO Box 2087
Santa Fe, New Mexico 87504
museumofnewmexicopress.org